THE SPIRITUAL GUIDANCE OF

THE INDIVIDUAL AND HUMANITY

THE SPIRITUAL GUIDANCE OF THE INDIVIDUAL AND HUMANITY

Some Results of Spiritual-Scientific Research into Human History and Development

RUDOLF STEINER

Translated by Samuel Desch

ⓔ ANTHROPOSOPHIC PRESS

This book is a translation of *Die geistige Führung des Menschen und der Menschheit* (volume 15 in the Collected Works), published by Rudolf Steiner Verlag, Dornach, Switzerland, 1974.

Published in the United States by Anthroposophic Press, R.R.4, Box 94 A1, Hudson, New York 12534.

Copyright © 1992 by Anthroposophic Press, Inc.

Library of Congress Cataloging-in-Publication Data

Steiner, Rudolf, 1861-1925.
  [Geistige Führung des Menschen und der Menschheit. English]
The spiritual guidance of the individual and humanity : some results of
spiritual-scientific research into human history and development /
Rudolf Steiner ; translated by Samuel Desch.
    Translation of: Die geistige Führung des Menschen und der Menschheit.
    Includes bibliographical references.
    ISBN 0-88010-364-7
    1. Anthroposophy. 2. Jesus Christ — Anthroposophical interpretations.
I. Title.
BP595.S894G4713   1992   92-3707
299'.935 — dc20   CIP

Cover Design by Barbara Richey and Mary Giddens.

10 9 8 7 6 5 4 3 2 1

All rights reserved. No part of this book may be reproduced in
any form without the written permission of the publisher, except
for brief quotations embodied in critical reviews and articles.

Printed in the United States of America.

CONTENTS

INTRODUCTION

This book is the first volume of a new edition of all Rudolf Steiner's written work — *Classics in Anthroposophy*. It can be called a classic for several reasons and it contains an important presentation of Rudolf Steiner's Christology (his research into the Christ impulse in earthly and cosmic evolution). It is one of the best accounts of this teaching with which to begin one's study, and one to which we can profitably return again and again.

Steiner had little time to revise his lectures — even during the early years of the century — due to the sheer magnitude of his lecturing activity, which increased each year; he sometimes gave two or more lectures in twenty-four hours. Today, about 6000 of these lectures are in print. In addition to his lectures, Steiner's days were filled with administrative and other teaching duties, as well as meeting the needs of people who sought his advice for personal concerns. The lectures in this book and those now published as *The Mission of the Individual Folk-souls* are the only lectures he was able to revise in all his years as a spiritual teacher. Rudolf Steiner often emphasized the qualitative difference between his written works and his lectures, which are unrevised stenographic reports. Indeed, he did not write many books, and most of those that he did write underwent at least one revision during his lifetime, as he sought constantly for the clarity and precision that epitomize his approach to spiritual science.

Originally he had not wanted the lectures to be published at all, but his students began to pass around lecture notes to facilitate their studies. One must imagine their excitement in those days, when each cycle of lectures seemed to present new revelations from Steiner's research. It was natural that those who could travel to various cities and attend the lectures wished to convey these esoteric treasures to their friends. On the other hand, Steiner lectured to specific audiences according to what he thought they needed to hear out of their karmic backgrounds, and many of the lectures that are now available to the general public were originally given for members of the Theosophical Society, and later, the Anthroposophical Society. Many listeners had been personal students of Steiner for some years and had become familiar with the general outlines of his teachings. In 1923, after the founding of the Anthroposophical Society, he decided to make all his lectures available to the public. The published lectures contained a note that some basic familiarity with fundamental anthroposophy was necessary for an intelligent reading, and that criticism not based on such knowledge would have to be disregarded.

Yet, in the case of this book, he undertook to revise the lectures he had given June 5-8, 1911 in Copenhagen. He spent about two weeks on the revision, and the lectures were printed only two months later, on August 26, 1911. In his preface, Steiner says there were reasons he allowed these lectures to appear when they did. We may ask what those reasons were.

Rudolf Steiner sought for many years a place where he could speak openly out of his spiritual insights. Accordingly, he accepted an invitation to lecture to the Berlin lodge of the Theosophical Society in 1900. The enthusiastic reception of these and other lectures led to his assuming the position of General Secretary of the German section of the Theosophical Society in 1902. From the beginning he asserted his intention to teach from the results of his own research in accordance with the needs of Western humanity, and this freedom was granted. Within the organizational framework of the Theosophical Society, Steiner worked to serve those souls who sought a spiritual impulse they could not find in either the sciences or in the established churches. For several years, Steiner's relationship with the Society was largely cordial and fruitful, and he lectured in many European cities to the lodges of the Theosophical Society.

The Theosophical Society took an increasingly Eastern direction, both spiritually and geographically. The headquarters was moved to Adyar, India. The leaders of the Theosophical Society, at first the remarkable Helena Petrovna Blavatsky, and then Annie Besant and Charles Leadbeater, as well as many members, had strong feelings against Western spirituality and the Christian churches. In 1911, Mrs. Besant proclaimed Jiddhu Krishnamurti, then a young boy, the incarnation of the Christ, and she created the Order of the Star of the East to promote this idea. This, of course, directly contradicted Rudolf Steiner's perception that the physical incarnation of Christ could occur only once during the history of the earth, for reasons carefully delineated in this book.

In 1912, some of the German members, opposed to the Order of the Star of the East, decided to form a new organization; Rudolf Steiner, when asked, offered the name "Anthroposophical Society." Steiner neither desired nor actively pursued the break with the theosophists but, recognizing that it was impossible to work within the increasingly hostile atmosphere of the Theosophical Society, he agreed to work with the new "anthroposophical" organization. The first meeting was held in 1913, after Mrs. Besant had excluded the German section. Readers new to anthroposophy may see these events as typical of the regrettable yet apparently inevitable infighting that occurs within spiritual organizations of all kinds. They take on a quite different coloring, however, when seen in the context of Steiner's struggle to insure that his unique teaching of Christian esotericism could find its proper audience and the necessary methods of presentation.[1]

Thus it was that Rudolf Steiner revised these lectures — an important element in the initial exposition of his Christology — during the height of difficulties within the Theosophical Society, just before the inauguration of the Anthroposophical Society. During these years he also wrote and produced his four mystery dramas, and began the work that later matured as eurythmy and speech formation.[2] Rudolf Steiner introduced something quite foreign to the mode of theosophical meetings when he began including artistic presentations in 1907. The effect of his dramas, which included eurythmy and the new method of speech, gave the impetus to create a special building in which to perform them. Looking back, we can see how Steiner's studies in Christology and his artistic work in drama, painting, and sculpture culminated in the building of the first Goetheanum in Dornach.[3]

It is not surprising, then, that *The Spiritual Guidance of the Individual and Humanity* reveals an extremely artistic composition. Rudolf Steiner weaves together the themes of the beings that guide humanity, the working of the Christ impulse before and after the Mystery of Golgotha, and our common soul experience in a way that can best be called musical. Each new expression brings a variation that imparts new information and yet relates to what precedes it. In some of his other lectures, Rudolf Steiner builds mighty pictures of the earth and of the cosmos, and portrays the activities of spiritual beings whose deeds are revealed externally through the natural sciences and through history. Until one achieves a sufficient background through contemplative study of a variety of anthroposophical concepts and makes the effort to allow these concepts to create the inner organs for further work, these initial studies can be overwhelming in their complexity and seem quite dry. For that reason, this book can be most helpful, because Steiner here relates the entire subject matter to the human soul, to observations and experiences we share as human beings. These can help us find an inner strength to begin to take anthroposophy more deeply into our own soul life.

The first lecture begins with a description of how, in the first three years of life, the higher self in each of us works to establish three capacities. Unlike the animals, we *learn* to orient our body in space in a way that is not innate or instinctual. Next, we learn to use language; and then comes the ability to work with thoughts, with ideas. Thus, in the time before we become aware of our "I", we have already done our wisest work on ourselves. If, however, our higher, divine self continued to work in this way, we would remain as children and not have the possibility of freedom. This active working must fall away as we achieve our own self-consciousness, which is constantly subject to the lure of pride and deceit, but which also gives us the possibility of self-development. Indeed, if the higher self lived within us in our present constitution for longer than three years, our body would die. In the same way, when the cosmic Christ entered the body of Jesus during the baptism in the Jordan, it could only live even in this special human body for three years.

Even if the Gospels had not been written, Steiner asserts, knowledge of the first years of childhood would reveal that Christ lives in us: "To perceive and understand the forces at work in our childhood is to perceive Christ in us." Through inner striving, we can contact again the wisdom that worked on us so powerfully in our first years, and we can find the Christ because of his incarnation into humanity. Indeed, the goal of earthly evolution, of the existence of this planet and our life on it, is to gradually make our entire being an expression of these divine cosmic forces — of the Christ impulse. Childhood is a perpetual reminder of the higher self, and it reveals the spiritual guidance that also lives in the Gospels and in the great initiates.

In the second lecture, Steiner describes humanity's own childlike condition in ancient times, and then he outlines how the higher spiritual beings have passed through their own "human" stage in earlier incarnations of the earth. As recently as ancient Egypt, people could recognize the spiritual beings who spoke through their leaders and teachers. The focus of the lecture is on the angels, the beings closest to humanity, who guided human development during the Egyptian epoch and again during our time. He shows how some of the angels have progressed properly in their development, while others have developed more slowly. These two types of angels bring to humanity both the possibility for our own progressive evolution, and also the two kinds of evil: the tendency to ignore our earthly responsibilities and become dreamers and visionaries, and the increasing temptation toward materialism. While their activities cause trouble in the present life of humanity, these beings actually work together in the spiritual world to guide human development. With delicacy and beauty, Steiner indicates the necessity for these retarding spirits in our evolution, for without them, we would not have the opportunity to achieve full self-consciousness, diversity, and freedom. The more progressive beings could only have produced uniformity in human nature.

This lecture concludes with a caution against fanaticism. "The most beautiful things can seduce and tempt us if we pursue them one-sidedly." To guard against this, he urges us to insure that clairvoyance is augmented by an effort to grasp conceptually just the kind of spiritual facts that are presented in this book. Spiritual science helps us to avoid error; clairvoyance should be accompanied by initiation, the training that allows "a clear assessment of what is perceived in the supersensible world." This is the difference between seeing and understanding, the ability to distinguish between the different kinds of beings and events of the higher worlds. Most importantly, through the study of anthroposophy, we begin to meet the Christ with our higher soul forces.

In the final lecture, Rudolf Steiner surveys the sweep of the post-Atlantean age, the present age of the world.[4] He shows how the progressive spiritual beings have also met the Christ, but the retarding beings have not. These latter spirits have inspired the natural science that has formed our present world culture. In the future, scientists will perceive that the Christ has arranged every atom of the earth, and a new physics and chemistry will result. We can say, then, that in the future there will live in people's hearts a Christ-idea whose magnitude will be beyond anything humanity has believed to know and understand so far. What has developed through Christ as a first impulse and has lived on as an idea of him until now is — even in the best representatives of the Christ-principle — only a preparation for a true understanding of Christ. Christ first entered human hearts through the pictures from his life on earth in a human body. Today we must prepare for a spiritual meeting with the Christ, similar to Paul's experience at Damascus. An essential part of this preparation is a strengthened consciousness and a sense of responsibility toward spiritual perception, and this vital discrimination can be enhanced through the careful study of such a book as this one.

In conclusion, one hopes that this new edition will find the active readership it deserves. Many people who approach anthroposophy for the first time are suspicious and even resentful of Christianity as it has manifested in the past two thousand years, and when they discover that anthroposophy is Christ-centered, they may feel disappointed or even upset. For others, it is perplexing that Steiner's Christology puts forward quite radical elements when compared to the theology of his day or ours. In this book, Rudolf Steiner gives both a broad, sweeping picture of human and cosmic evolution and the central place of the Christ impulse in that development, and also relates this evolution to our inner life, to the experiences and insights that anyone with the good will to look within can have, and from which they can then follow these anthroposophical thoughts to the reality of the Christ experience. Here we are given a deeply rewarding perspective of the age in which we live and in which we are witnessing the rapid dissolution of our cultural life; here also we can find the inner sustenance to work toward building the culture of a new age. From this point of view *The Spiritual Guidance of the Individual and Humanity* is a "classic" work of spiritual science.

HILMAR MOORE

Notes

1. For further information, see Guenther Wachsmuth, *The Life and Work of Rudolf Steiner* (Whittier Books, 1955) 158–193; and Stewart C. Easton, *Rudolf Steiner: Herald of a New Epoch* (Anthroposophic Press, 1980), chapters 6 and 8. It should be noted that Krishnamurti publicly repudiated the claims of Besant and Leadbeater and dissolved the organization, called the Order of the Star of the East, in the 1920s. Stewart Easton has managed to portray with admirable clarity the issues and personalities that are of great importance in Steiner's work. In chapter 5 of his *Man and World in the Light of Anthroposophy* (Anthroposophic Press, 1975) he has provided a succinct presentation of Rudolf Steiner's Christology.

2. Eurythmy. System of movement created by Rudolf Steiner expressing both music and the sounds of speech. See Marjorie Raffe et al., *Eurythmy and the Impulse of Dance*, (London: Rudolf Steiner Press, 1974).

Speech. Steiner developed a particular mode of artistic speech in the production of his Mystery Dramas. See Rudolf Steiner, *Speech and Drama*, (Spring Valley, NY: Anthroposophic Press/London: Rudolf Steiner Press, 1968). Also, Steiner, *Four Mystery Dramas*, trans. Ruth Pusch, (North Vancouver: Steiner Book Centre, 1973) and Steiner, *Three Lectures on the Mystery Dramas*, (Spring Valley, NY: Anthroposophic Press, 1983).

3. The Goetheanum is the world headquarters of the Anthroposophical Society in Dornach, Switzerland. Architecturally unique. See Biesantz, *The Goetheanum*, (London: Rudolf Steiner Press, 1979) and Rex Raab et al., *Eloquent Concrete*, (London: Rudolf Steiner Press, 1979).

4. For a description of earth evolution, including post-Atlantean times, see Rudolf Steiner, *An Outline of Occult Science*, 3rd edition., repr., (Hudson, NY: Anthropsophic Press, 1989).

PREFACE

This book reproduces the content of lectures I gave in June of this year in Copenhagen on the occasion of the General Assembly of the Scandinavian Theosophical Society. They were delivered to an audience familiar with spiritual science or theosophy [anthroposophy], and thus they presuppose this familiarity.[1] They are in every detail based on my books *Theosophy* and *An Outline of Occult Science*.[2] Anyone unacquainted with the premises of these books would certainly regard this report as a curious product of mere fantasy. However, the above mentioned books present the scientific basis for everything said here.

I have completely revised the stenographic transcription of the lectures, but my intention in publishing them was to retain, as much as possible, the character of the original spoken presentation. This should be noted here because it is my opinion that a discourse intended for reading must be completely different from a spoken one. I have followed this principle in all my previous writings that were intended for publication. The style and presentation of this book are closer to the spoken word because I have reasons for allowing this account to be published at this time and because a complete revision in accordance with the above principle would take a very long time.

RUDOLF STEINER
Munich, August 20, 1911

LECTURE ONE

IF WE REFLECT upon ourselves, we soon come to realize that, in addition to the self we encompass with our thoughts, feelings, and fully conscious impulses of will, we bear in ourselves a second, more powerful self. We become aware that we subordinate ourselves to this second self as to a higher power. At first, this second self seems to us a lower being when compared to the one we encompass with our clear, fully conscious soul and its natural inclination toward the good and the true. And so, initially, we may strive to overcome this seemingly lower self.

A closer self-examination, however, can teach us something else about this second self. If periodically we look back on what we have experienced or done in life, we make a strange discovery, one that becomes more meaningful for us the older we become. Whenever we think about what we did or said at some time in the past, it turns out that we did a great many things we actually understood only at a later date. When we think of things we did seven or eight years ago — or perhaps even twenty years ago — we realize that only now, after a long time, is our mind sufficiently developed to understand what we did or said then.

Of course, there are people who do not make such self-discoveries because they do not try to. Nevertheless, this sort of soul-searching is extraordinarily fruitful. For in such moments as we become aware that we are only now beginning to understand something we did in our earlier years — that in the past our minds were not mature enough to understand what we did or said then — a new feeling emerges in our soul. We feel ourselves as if sheltered by a benevolent power presiding in the depths of our own being. We begin to trust more and more that, in the highest sense of the word, we are not alone in the world and that whatever we can understand or do consciously is fundamentally only a small part of what we accomplish in the world.

After we have gone through this process of discovery a number of times, an insight that is theoretically easy to understand can become part of our practical lives. We know, in theory at any rate, that we would not get very far in life if we had to do everything in full consciousness, rationally understanding all the circumstances and ramifications in every case. To see that this is so we need only consider how and when we accomplish those acts that are the wisest and most important for our existence. A moment's thought will reveal that we act most wisely in the time between birth and the moment at which memory, that first moment we can remember when in later years we try to recall our early life, begins.

This is to say that, as we think back to what we did three, four, or five and more years ago, we reach a certain point in childhood beyond which our memory does not extend. Our memory does not go back any further. Parents or other people can tell us what happened before that time, but our own memory does not go back beyond a certain point. This is the point in our lives when we first began to perceive ourselves as an *I*. People whose memory is intact can usually remember back to, but not earlier than, this moment.

Our souls, however, have already performed their wisest deeds *before* this time. Never again in later life, after we have attained full consciousness, will we be able to accomplish such splendid and tremendous deeds as those we accomplished out of the unconscious depths of our souls in the first years of childhood.

As we know, we bring the fruits of earlier lives on earth with us into the physical world at birth. For example, at birth our physical brain is still an incomplete and unfinished instrument. The soul must then work on it, adding the finer, detailed structures that make it the medium of all the soul's faculties. In fact, before the soul is fully conscious, it works on the brain to transform it into an instrument to express all the capacities, aptitudes, characteristics, and so on, that it has as a consequence of earlier lives. This work on our own body is guided from a perspective that is wiser than anything we can achieve later with our full consciousness. Moreover, during this time when the brain is being transformed, we must also acquire the three most important capacities for life on earth.

The first capacity we must learn is to *orient* our body in space. People today do not realize what this means and that it touches on the most essential differences between human beings and animals. Animals are destined from the beginning to achieve their equilibrium in a certain way: one is destined to be a climber, another a swimmer, and so on. Animals are so constituted that from the outset they can orient themselves in space correctly. This is true even of primates. If zoologists were aware of this, they would put less emphasis on the number of similar bones, muscles, and so forth that human beings and animals have. After all, this is not nearly as important as the fact that human beings are not given an innate way to achieve equilibrium in space but must develop it out of their total being.[1]

It is significant that we must work on ourselves to develop from beings that cannot walk into ones that walk upright. We achieve our vertical position, our position of equilibrium in space, by ourselves. In other words, we establish our own relationship to gravity. Those who do not wish to consider the question deeply will, of course, easily dispute our explanation on apparently good grounds. They may claim, for example, that we are just as well constituted for walking upright as climbing animals are for climbing. Upon closer examination, however, we find that animals' orientation in space is determined by their physical organization. In human beings, however, it is the soul that establishes the relationship to space and shapes the organization.

The second capacity we learn out of ourselves from our essential being — which remains the same through successive incarnations — is *language*. This allows us to relate to our fellow human beings and makes us bearers of the spiritual life that permeates the physical world primarily by means of human beings. It has often been emphasized, and with good reason, that someone stranded on a desert island who had had no contact with other human beings before learning to speak would never learn to do so. What we receive through heredity, on the other hand, what is implanted in us for development in later years, does not depend on our interactions with other human beings. For example, we are predisposed by heredity to change teeth in our seventh year. Even on a desert island our second set of teeth would grow if we reached that age. But if our soul being, the part of us that continues from one life to the next, is not stimulated we will not learn to speak. In a sense, we must sow the seed for the development of the larynx in the time before our earliest memory — before we attain full I-consciousness — so that the larynx can then become an organ of speech.

There is still a third, even less well known, capacity that we learn on our own through what we bear within us through successive incarnations. I am referring here to our ability to live within the world of thoughts and ideas, the world of thought itself. Our brain is formed and worked on because it is the tool of *thinking*. At the beginning of life, the brain is still malleable because we must shape it ourselves to make it an instrument for the thinking appropriate to our essential being. The brain at birth is the result of the work of forces inherited from our parents, grandparents, and so on. It is in our thinking that we bring to expression what we are as individuals in conformity with our former earthly lives. Therefore, after birth, when we have become physically independent of our parents and ancestors, we must transform the brain we have inherited.

Clearly, then, we accomplish significant steps in the early years of life. We work on ourselves in accordance with the highest wisdom. In fact, if we had to rely on our own intelligence, we could not achieve what we must accomplish *without* our intelligence in the first few years of our lives. Why is this so? Why must all these things be accomplished from soul depths that lie *outside* our consciousness? Because, in the first years of our lives, our souls, as well as our whole being, are much more closely connected with the spiritual worlds of the higher hierarchies than is the case later.

Clairvoyants, who can trace the spiritual processes involved because they have undergone spiritual training, discover that something tremendously significant happens at the moment when we achieve I-consciousness, that is, at the moment of our earliest memory. They can see that, during the early years of childhood, an aura hovers about us like a wonderful human-superhuman power. This aura, which is actually our higher part, extends everywhere into the spiritual world. But at the earliest moment we can remember, this aura penetrates more deeply into our inner being.[2] We can experience ourselves as a coherent I from this point on because what had previously been connected to the higher worlds then entered the I. Thereafter, our consciousness establishes its own relationship to the outer world.

This conscious relationship to the outer world does not yet exist in early childhood. In childhood, a dream world still seems to hover about us. We work on ourselves with a wisdom that is *not* in us, a wisdom that is more powerful and comprehensive than all the conscious wisdom we acquire later. This higher wisdom works from the spiritual world deep into the body; it enables us to form the brain out of the spirit. We can rightly say, then, that even the wisest person can learn from a child. For the wisdom at work in children does not become part of our consciousness in later life. It is obscured and exchanged for consciousness.

In the first years of life, however, this higher wisdom functions like a "telephone connection" to the spiritual beings in whose world we find ourselves between death and rebirth. Something from this world still flows into our aura during childhood. As individuals we are then directly subject to the guidance of the *entire* spiritual world to which we belong. When we are children — up to the moment of our earliest memory — the spiritual forces from this world flow into us, enabling us to develop our particular relationship to gravity. At the same time, the same forces also form our larynx and shape our brain into living organs for the expression of thought, feeling, and will.

During childhood, then, we work out of a self that is still in direct contact with the higher worlds. Indeed, to a certain degree, we can still do this even in later life, although conditions change. Whenever we feel that we did or said something in earlier years that we are only now coming to understand, we have an indication that we were guided by a higher wisdom at that earlier time. Only years later do we manage to gain insight into the motives of our past conduct. All this indicates that at birth we did not entirely leave behind the world we lived in before entering into our new, physical existence. In fact, we never leave it behind completely. What we have as our part of higher spirituality enters our physical life and remains with us. Thus, what we bear within us is not a higher self that has to be developed gradually, but one that already exists and that often leads us to rise above ourselves.

All that we can produce in the way of ideals and artistic creativity — as also the natural healing forces in our body, which continuously compensate for the injuries life inflicts — originate not in our ordinary, rational minds but in the deeper forces that work in our early years on our orientation in space, on the formation of the larynx, and on the development of the brain. These same forces are still present in us later. People often say of the damages and injuries we sustain in life that external forces will not be of any help and that our organism must develop its own inherent healing powers. What they are talking about is a wise, benevolent influence working upon us. From this same source also arise the best forces that enable us to perceive the spiritual world — that is, to have true clairvoyance.

We can now ask why the higher powers work on us only in the early years of childhood. It is easy to answer one half of this question, for if these higher forces continued to work on us in the same way into later life, we would always remain children and could never achieve full I-consciousness. What worked previously from without must be transferred into our own being.

But there is a more significant reason, one that can tell us more about the mysteries of human life. Spiritual science teaches that we have to consider the human body at the present stage of the earth's evolution as having developed from earlier conditions. People familiar with spiritual science know that in the course of this evolution various forces have worked on our whole being—some on the physical body, others on the etheric body, and others again on the astral body.[3] We have evolved to our present condition because beings we call *luciferic* and *ahrimanic* have affected us. Through their forces, our essential being became worse than it would have been if only the forces of the spiritual guides of the world, those who want to advance our development in a straight line, had worked on us. Indeed, suffering, disease, and death can be traced to the fact that, in addition to the beings who advance our development in a straight line, luciferic and ahrimanic beings are also at work and continuously thwart our progress.

What we bring with us at birth contains something that is better than anything we can make of it in later life. In early childhood, the luciferic and ahrimanic forces have only a limited influence on our being. Essentially, they are active only in what we make of ourselves through our conscious life. If we retained the best part of ourselves in its full force beyond the first phase of childhood, its influence would be too much for us because the luciferic and ahrimanic forces opposing the part of ourselves that is better than the rest would weaken our whole being. Our constitution as human beings in the physical world is such that, once we are no longer soft and malleable as children, we can no longer stand to have the forces of the spiritual world continue to affect us directly. The forces that underlie our orientation in space and the formation of the larynx and the brain would shatter us if they continued to influence us directly in later life. These forces are so powerful that our organism would waste away beneath their holiness if they continued to work on us. However, for the activity that brings us into conscious contact with the supersensible world, we have to call upon these forces again.

This leads us to a realization that is very significant if we understand it rightly. In the New Testament it is put thus: "Unless you turn and become like children, you will never enter the kingdom of heaven." (Matthew 18:3) What then seems to be the highest ideal for a human being if the above statement is correctly understood? Surely that our ideal must be to approach ever closer a conscious relationship with the forces that worked on us, without our awareness, in the first years of childhood. At the same time, we must realize that we would collapse under the power of these forces if they were *immediately and too easily* to affect our conscious life. That is why a careful preparation is necessary to achieve the capacities that lead to a perception of supersensible worlds. The goal of this preparation is to enable us to bear what we simply cannot bear in ordinary life.

* * *

Our passing through successive incarnations is significant for the overall evolution of our essential being, which has undergone successive past lives and will continue to go through future lives. The evolution of the earth runs parallel to our own. At some point in the future, the earth will have reached the end of its course; then the planet earth, as a physical entity, will have to separate from the totality of human souls — just as when we die the body separates from the spirit, and the soul, in order to live on, enters the spiritual realm between death and rebirth.[4] From this point of view, our highest ideal must be the striving to make all the fruits to be gained in earthly life truly our own before we die.

The forces that make us too weak to bear those forces that work on us in childhood originate in the organism of the earth. By the time this separates from humanity, we must have advanced to the point of giving over our whole being to the forces that presently work on us only in childhood. Only when we have reached this level can we claim to have attained our goal. Thus, through successive earthly lives, we must gradually make our entire being, including our consciousness, an expression of the forces that work on us under the guidance of the spiritual world in early childhood. This is the purpose of evolution.

After such considerations, the realization that we are not alone takes hold of our soul. This realization imbues us with humility, but also with a proper consciousness of our human dignity. We realize at the same time that something lives in us that can prove at all times that we can rise above ourselves to a self that is already surpassing us and

will continue to do so from one life to the next. As this realization assumes a more and more definite form, it can
have a very soothing, heartwarming effect and, at the
same time, imbue the soul with the appropriate humility
and modesty. What lives within us is truly a higher, divine human being, and we can feel ourselves pervaded by
this being as by a living presence of whom we can say,
This is my inner guide in me.

Given this, the thought easily arises that we should
strive in every way possible to achieve harmony with that
part in us that is wiser than our conscious intelligence.
Thereafter, our attention will no longer be directed to the
conscious self but will be focused instead on an expanded
self, and from this perspective we can then combat and
eradicate all our false pride and arrogance. From this feeling we will gradually come to a right understanding of
our present incompleteness. We shall come to see that we
will become complete when the comprehensive spirituality at work in us has the same relationship to our adult
consciousness that it had to our unconscious soul life in
early childhood.

Even though we may not remember anything from our
first four years of life, we can safely say that the active influence of the higher spiritual realms lasts for about the
first three years. By the end of this period we have become able to connect the impressions from the outer
world with our I-concept. To be sure, this coherent I-concept cannot be traced back beyond the first moment we
can remember. This is a moment that is difficult to locate,
for with the awakening of distinct I-consciousness, our

memory may be so weak that it cannot be recovered later. Nevertheless, we may say that people generally remember as far back as the beginning of the fourth year. In other words, we are justified in saying that the higher forces that have a decisive influence on us in childhood can work on us for *three years*. It follows that our constitution in the present, middle phase of the earth's evolution enables us to absorb these higher forces for only three years.

Now if, through some special cosmic powers, we could somehow remove the ordinary I from a person — if the ordinary I that has accompanied a person through successive incarnations could be separated from that person's physical, etheric, and astral bodies — and we could then replace the ordinary I with an I that is connected with the spiritual worlds — what would happen? After three years this person's body would fall apart! If such a thing were to happen, world karma would have to do something to prevent the spiritual being connected to the higher worlds from living in this body for more than three years.* Only at the conclusion of our earthly lives will we be able to retain the forces within ourselves that allow us to live with that spiritual being for more than three years. Then we will be able to say, *Not I but this higher self in me, which has been there all along, is now at work in me.* Until then, we will not be able to experience this. At most, we will be able to feel the presence of this higher self, but

---

*During the transition from childhood to the following stages, our organism retains its viability because it can still change during this period. In later life it can no longer change, and therefore cannot survive with the self connected directly to the spiritual worlds.

our actual, real human I will not yet be able to bring the higher self fully to life.

Let us now assume that a human organism were to enter the world at some moment in the middle of the earth's lifetime, and that, at a certain point by means of certain cosmic powers, this organism was freed of its I and received in its stead the I that is usually active only in the first three years of childhood — the I that is connected to the spiritual worlds we live in between death and rebirth. How long would such a person be able to live in an earthly body? Such a person would be able to survive in this earthly body only for about three years. After three years, world karma would have to intervene and destroy this human organism.

What we have assumed here did actually occur at one time in history. When the human organism known as Jesus stood on the banks of the Jordan to be baptized by John, his I left his physical, etheric, and astral bodies. But after the Baptism, that organism bore within itself the higher self of humanity in fully conscious form. The self that works on us with cosmic wisdom in childhood, before we are conscious of it, was then fully conscious in Jesus of Nazareth. And by this very fact, this self, which was connected to the higher spiritual world, could live in this human body for only three years. Events then had to follow a course that brought an end to Jesus' physical life three years after the Baptism.

Indeed, we have to understand the external events in the life of Jesus Christ as resulting from the inner causes discussed above. They are the *outer expression* of these causes. This reveals the deeper connection between the guide in us — which radiates into our childhood as into a dark room and always works under the surface of our consciousness as our best self — and what once entered into human history to live for three years in a human sheath.

This "higher" I, which is connected to the spiritual hierarchies, entered history in the person of Jesus of Nazareth — an event that is symbolized by the spirit descending in the form of a dove, saying: "This is my well beloved Son, today I have begotten him" (Matthew 3:17). (Such is the original meaning of the words). What is revealed here? If we hold this image of the Baptism before our eyes, we have before us the highest human ideal. That is what is meant when the gospels tell us that Christ can be seen and known in every person. Even if there were no gospels and no tradition to report that a Christ once lived, our knowledge of the nature of the human being would tell us that Christ is alive in us.

To know the forces at work in childhood is to know the Christ in us. The question then arises whether this realization also leads us to acknowledge that Christ at one time really lived on earth in a human body? We can answer "yes" to this without requiring any documents, because true clairvoyant self-knowledge convinces people in our time that there are forces *in the human soul* that come from Christ.

In the first three years of childhood these forces are active without any effort on our part. They can also work on us in our later life — if we seek Christ in ourselves through contemplation. It was not always possible to find the

Christ within; indeed, as clairvoyant perception reveals, prior to Christ's life on earth, there were times when no amount of contemplation would have helped people to find the Christ. Clairvoyant cognition teaches us that this is so. Between the time when Christ could not be found within and the present, when he can be found in this way, lies Christ's life on earth. It is because Christ lived on the earth that we can now find him within, in the way I have indicated. Thus, for clairvoyant perception, the fact that Christ lived on the earth is proven without recourse to any historical documentation.

It is as if Christ had said: Human beings, I want to be an ideal for you that presents to you on a higher, spiritual level what is fulfilled in the body. In the early years of life we learn out of the spirit, first, to walk — that is, we learn, under the guidance of the spirit, to find our *way* in earthly life. Then we learn to speak — to formulate the *truth* — out of the spirit. In other words, we develop the essence of truth out of speech sounds. Finally, we also develop the organ for our *life* as earthly I-beings. Thus, in the first three years of life, we learn three things. We learn to find the "way," that is, to walk; we learn to represent the "truth" with our organism, and we learn to express "life" in our body through the spirit. There is no more meaningful paraphrase imaginable of the words "Unless you turn and become like children, you will never enter the kingdom of heaven." (Matthew 18:3)

Most meaningfully, therefore, the I-being of Christ is expressed in the words: *"I am the Way, the Truth, and the Life!"* The higher spiritual forces form our organism in childhood — though we are not conscious of this — so that our body becomes the expression of the way, the truth, and the life. Similarly, the human spirit gradually becomes the *conscious* bearer of the way, the truth, and the life by permeating itself with Christ. Thereby we transform ourselves in the course of our earthly life into the power at work in us in childhood.

Words such as these about the way, the truth, and the life can open the doors of eternity for us. Once our self-knowledge has become true and substantial, these words will resound for us from the depths of our soul.

What I have presented here opens up a twofold perspective on the spiritual guidance of the individual and of humanity as a whole. First, as individuals, we find the Christ, the guide in us, through self-knowledge. We can always find Christ in this way because, since his life on earth, he is always present in us. Second, when we apply the knowledge we have gained without the help of historical documents to these documents, we begin to understand their true nature. They are the historical expression of something that has revealed itself in the depths of the soul. Therefore, historical documents should be regarded as part of that guidance of humanity that is intended to lead the soul to itself.

If we understand the eternal spirit of the words "I am the Way, the Truth, and the Life" in this way, we do not need to ask why we have to enter life as children even after having passed through many incarnations. For we realize that this apparent imperfection is a perpetual reminder of the highest that lives in us. We cannot be reminded often enough — we need to be reminded at least at the beginning of each new life — of the great truth of what we really are in our innermost essential being, that underlies all our earthly lives but remains untouched by the imperfections of earthly existence.

It is best not to present too many definitions or concepts when talking about spiritual science or theosophy [anthroposophy] or about occultism in general. It is better to describe things and to try to convey an idea of what they really are like. That is why I have tried here to give you a sense of what is characteristic of the first three years of life and of how this relates to the light that radiates from the cross on Golgotha. The description I have given bespeaks an impulse in human evolution that will make St. Paul's words "Not I, but Christ in me" come true. All we need to know is what as human beings we really are; on the basis of this knowledge we can then gain insight into the being of Christ. Only after we have arrived at this Christ-idea through a real understanding of humanity, and after we have understood that to find Christ we must seek him in ourselves, will turning to the Bible be useful for us. No one has a greater or more conscious appreciation of the Bible than those who have found Christ in this way.

Imagine that a Martian who had never heard anything about Christ and his works, came down to earth. This Martian would not understand much of what happened here, and much of what interests people today would not interest this visitor. However, this Martian would be interested in what is the central impulse of earthly evolution, namely, the Christ-idea as expressed in human nature. Once we understand this, we will for the first time be able to read the Bible correctly, for we will then see that it expresses in a wonderful way what we have first perceived within ourselves. You see, we do not need to be taught a particular appreciation of the gospels. When we read the gospels as fully conscious individuals, what we have learned through spiritual science enables us to fully realize their greatness.

I am hardly exaggerating when I claim that there will come a time when the general opinion will be that people who have learned to understand and appreciate the content of the gospels through spiritual science will see them as scriptures intended for the guidance of humanity and that their understanding will do the Bible more justice than anything else has so far. It is only through understanding our own inner being that we can come to see what lies hidden in these profound scriptures. Now, if we find in the gospels what is so completely part of our own being, it follows that it must have entered the scriptures through the people who wrote them. Thus, what we have to admit concerning ourselves — and the older we get, the more often we have to admit it — namely, that we do many things we don't understand fully until many years later: this must also be true for the writers of the gospels. They wrote out of the higher self that works on all of us in childhood. Thus, the gospels originate in the same wisdom that forms us. The spirit is revealed physically in the human body as well as in the writing of the gospels.

In this context, the concept of inspiration becomes meaningful once again in a positive sense. Just as higher forces work on the brain in the first three years of child-hood, so the spiritual worlds imbued the writers of the gospels with the forces out of which they wrote their gospels. These facts reveal the spiritual guidance of humanity. After all, if there are people in the human race who write documents out of the same forces that wisely shape human beings, then humanity as a whole is truly being *guided*. And just as individuals say or do things they understand only at a later age, so humanity as a whole produced evangelists as mediators who provided revelations that can be understood only gradually. These scriptures will be understood more and more as humanity progresses. As individuals, we can feel a spiritual guid-ance within us; humanity as a whole can feel it in persons who work as the gospel writers did.

The concept of the guidance of humanity we have just established can now be expanded in many ways. Let us assume a person has found students or disciples, that is, people who declare their faith in him and become his loy-al followers. Such a person out of genuine self-knowl-edge will easily realize that having found students gives him the feeling that what he has to say does not originate within him. Instead, spiritual forces from higher worlds want to communicate with the students and find in the teacher a suitable instrument for revealing themselves.

Such a teacher may then reason as follows: When I was a child, I worked on myself by means of forces that came from the spiritual world. The best I can now con-tribute here must also come from higher worlds. I must not consider it as part of my ordinary consciousness.

Indeed, such an individual may feel that something like a *daemon* — the word *daemon* here refers to a benevolent spiritual power — works from the spiritual world through him on the students.

According to Plato, Socrates felt something like this when he spoke of his *daemon* as something that guided and directed him.[5] Many attempts have been made to explain Socrates' *daemon*. However, to explain it we must accept the idea that Socrates could feel something akin to what emerges from the above considerations. Based on this, we then realize that during the three or four centuries when the Socratic principle prevailed in Greece, Socrates introduced a mood into the Greek world that served as preparation for another great event. The mood I am referring to accompanied the realization that what we perceive of an individual does not comprise the whole of what enters this world from the higher one. This mood continued to prevail long after Socrates' death. The best people who had this feeling later also best understood the words "Not I, but the Christ in me." They realized that Socrates had to speak of a *daemon-like* force working out of the higher worlds, but through the ideal of Christ it became clear what Socrates had really meant. Of course, Socrates could not yet speak of Christ because in his time people could not yet find the Christ-being *within*.

Here again we feel something of a *spiritual* guidance of humanity; nothing can enter the world without preparation. Why did Paul find his best followers in Greece? Because Socratism had prepared the ground there. That is, more recent events in the development of humanity can be traced back to earlier events that prepared people to allow the later events to work upon them. This gives us an idea of how *far* the guiding impulse of human evolution reaches; it puts the right people at the right time in the place where they are needed for our development. In facts such as these the guidance of humanity is evident in a general way.

LECTURE TWO

WE CAN FIND an interesting parallel between what is revealed in the life of the individual and what rules in the development of humanity as a whole if we consider, for example, what the teachers and leaders of ancient Egypt told the Greeks about the guidance and direction of Egyptian spiritual life. The story is told that when an Egyptian was asked who had guided and led his people since ancient times, he answered that in remote antiquity *gods* had ruled and taught them and that only later did human beings become their leaders. He added that the first leader they acknowledged on the physical plane as a human-like being rather than a god was called Menes.[1] In other words, according to Greek accounts, the Egyptian leaders asserted that the gods themselves had guided and directed their people in earlier times.

We must always take care to understand in the right way reports that have been handed down to us from ancient times. We need to think carefully about what the ancient Egyptians meant when they said that the gods had been their kings and great teachers. They meant that in ancient times those people who felt in their souls a kind of higher consciousness, a wisdom from higher worlds, had to put themselves into a clairvoyant state before they could find their true inspirer and teacher, for their true teacher would approach them only when their spiritual eyes were opened. Such a person when asked, "Who is your teacher?" would not have pointed to this or that individual, but would have entered a clairvoyant state — and we know from spiritual science that it was easier to achieve a clairvoyant state in ancient times than it is today. In that clairvoyant state, a person would have met his teacher, for in those days beings came down from the spiritual worlds who did not become incarnate in human bodies. Thus, in the remote past of ancient Egypt, the gods still ruled and taught, using human beings as their channels. At that time, however, the term "gods" referred to beings who had preceded human beings in their development.

Spiritual science teaches us that before becoming the "earth" as we know it today, the earth passed through an earlier planetary state or condition called the "moon state."[2] During this moon state, human beings were not yet human in our sense of the word. Nevertheless, there were other beings on the old Moon who had evolved to the same level as humans have now reached on the earth, though they looked very different from us. In other words, on the old Moon, which perished and later developed into our earth, there were beings we can consider as our forerunners. In Christian esotericism these beings are called *angeloi* (angels), while those beings above them, who reached the human stage of their development even earlier than the angels, are called *archangeloi* (archangels).

The *angeloi*, known as *dhyanic beings* or *dhyani* in oriental mysticism, reached the human level of their development during the Moon stage. Consequently, if they completed their evolution on the old Moon, they are now one level above us. At the end of earthly evolution, we will arrive at the level they reached at the end of the moon stage.

When the earth state of our planet began and human beings appeared on it, the angels could not manifest in outer human form because the human flesh body is essentially an earthly product appropriate only for beings now at the human stage of development. Since the angels are a level above the human, they could not incarnate in human bodies; they could participate in the government of the earth only by enlightening and inspiring human beings who had achieved a state of clairvoyance. These higher, angelic beings used clairvoyant individuals to intervene in the guidance of the earth's destiny. Thus the ancient Egyptians still remembered a time when their leaders were vividly conscious of their connection with these higher beings, called variously gods, angels, or dhyanic beings. These beings who influenced humanity without incarnating in human bodies, without taking on fleshly human form, were our forerunners; they had already outgrown the level of development we have reached only now.

The word "superhuman"[3] is often misused these days, but in this case we can use it correctly and apply it to those beings who had already achieved the human level of development during the moon period—the planetary stage preliminary to our earth—and have now grown beyond it. Such beings could appear on earth only in an etheric body and thus could be perceived only by clairvoyant individuals.[4] That is how they came down to earth from the spiritual worlds and ruled on the earth even in post-Atlantean times.[5]

These beings had the remarkable characteristic—indeed they still have it today—that they did not need to think. In fact, it may be said that they cannot think at all the way we do. After all, *how* do we think? Well, usually we start from a particular point, and once we have understood it, we try to comprehend other things on the basis of this understanding. If our thinking did not follow this pattern, many people would have an easier time learning in school. Mathematics, for example, cannot be learned in a day because we must begin at one point and proceed slowly from there. This takes a long time. An entire world of ideas cannot be taken in at a glance because human thinking takes its course *over time*. A complex thought structure cannot be present in the mind all at once; rather, we must make an effort to follow it step by step.

The higher beings I have described are not encumbered by this peculiar characteristic of human thinking. Instead, they realize an extensive train of thought as quickly as animals know to grab something the moment their instinct tells them it is edible. In higher beings, then, instinct and reflective consciousness are one and the same. What instincts are for animals at their evolutionary level, in their kingdom, direct spiritual thinking, or direct spiritual conceptualization, is for these dhyanic beings or angels. And this instinctive, conceptualizing inner life is what makes these higher beings so essentially different from us.

Obviously, the angeloi cannot possibly use the kind of brain or physical body we have. They must use an etheric body because the human body and brain can process thoughts only over time. The angeloi do not form their thoughts over time; they feel their wisdom flash up in them by itself, as it were. They cannot possibly make mistakes in their thinking the way we can. Their thinking is a direct inspiration. The individuals who were able to approach these superhuman or angelic beings were therefore aware of being in the presence of sure and reliable wisdom.

In ancient Egypt, then, those who were teachers or rulers knew that the commandments which their spiritual guides gave them and the truths they uttered were *immediately* right and could not be wrong. And the people to whom these truths were then imparted felt the same way. The clairvoyant leaders of ancient times could speak in such a way that the people believed that their words came from the spiritual world. In short, there was a direct current flowing down from the higher, guiding spiritual hierarchies.

Thus, the next higher world of the spiritual hierarchies guides the entire evolution of humanity; it works both on the individual in childhood and on humanity as a whole. The angeloi or superhuman beings of this realm are one level above us and reach directly up into the spiritual spheres. From these spheres they bring to earth what works into human culture. In the individual, this higher wisdom leaves its imprint on the formation of the body during childhood, and it formed the culture of ancient humanity in a similar way.

This is how the Egyptians, who reported that they were in contact with the divine realm, experienced the openness of the human soul to the spiritual hierarchies. Just as the child's soul opens its aura to the hierarchies until the moment indicated in the previous lecture, so, through its work, humanity as a whole opened its world to the hierarchies with which it was connected.

This connection to the higher hierarchies was particularly significant in the case of the holy teachers of India. These were the great teachers of the first post-Atlantean epoch, of the first Indian culture that spread in the south of Asia. After the end of the Atlantean catastrophe, when the physiognomy of the earth had changed and Asia, Europe, and Africa had developed in the eastern hemisphere in their new form, but before the time documented in ancient records, the culture of the ancient teachers of India flourished.

People today generally have a completely false picture of these great Indian teachers. If, for example, an educated person of our time were to meet one of the great teachers of India, he or she would look puzzled and probably say, "This is supposed to be a *wise* man? That is not how I imagined a wise man." According to our current definition of the terms "clever" and "intelligent," the ancient holy teachers of India would not have been able to say anything intelligent. By today's standards, these teachers were simple and very plain people who would have given the simplest answers to questions, even to questions pertaining to everyday life. Often, it was scarcely possible to elicit anything from them other than some sparse utterance that would seem quite insignificant to the educated classes of our day.

However, at certain times, these holy teachers proved to be more than merely simple people. At these times they had to gather in groups of seven, because what each could sense individually had to harmonize as if in a seven-tone harmony with what the other six experienced. Each wise man was able to perceive this or that, depending on his particular faculties and development. And out of the harmony of the individual perceptions of these seven individuals, there emerged the primeval wisdom that resounds through ancient times. Its reverberation can be heard even today if we decipher the occult records correctly. The records I am referring to are not the revelations of the Vedas, though the Vedas are certainly marvelous in their own right.[6] The teachings of these holy men of ancient India precede the writing of the Vedas by a long time. The Vedas, those tremendous works, are only a faint echo of those earlier teachings.

When these wise teachers faced one of the angeloi or superhuman forerunners of humanity, and looked clairvoyantly into the higher worlds, listening all the while clairaudiently to this being, their eyes shone like the sun. And what they were able to impart then had an awe inspiring effect on the people around them; all who heard them knew that they were not speaking out of human wisdom or human experience, but that *gods*, superhuman beings, were intervening in human culture.

The ancient cultures originated from this influx of divine wisdom. The gate to the divine-spiritual world was completely open for the human soul during Atlantean times. In the course of the post-Atlantean periods, however, gradually the gate closed. Little by little, people in many countries felt that human beings had to rely more and more on themselves. Here we can see again that the development of humanity as a whole parallels that of the child. At first the divine-spiritual world still extends into the child's unconscious soul, which is active in the formation of the body. Then comes the moment when each person begins to perceive himself or herself as an I, the first moment one can remember. Before this lies a time we cannot in any ordinary way usually recall. This is why it is said that even the wisest among us can still learn something from the soul of the child as it is in the time before memory develops. Thereafter, the individual is left to his or her own devices; I-consciousness appears, and we become able to remember our experiences.

In the same way there came a time when nations began to feel themselves cut off from the divine inspiration of their forefathers. For just as we are separated more and more from the aura guiding us during our early childhood years, so in the life of nations the divine forebearers gradually and increasingly withdrew. As a result, human beings were left to their own research and their own knowledge. In historical records that describe this development, we can feel the intervention of the guides of humanity.

The ancient Egyptians called the first founder of culture, who was human rather than divine, "Menes." And they dated the human possibility of *error* from the same moment, because from then on human beings had to rely on the instrument of the brain. The ancient Orientals likewise gave the name "Manes" to the human being as thinker and called the first bearer of human thinking "Manu." The Greeks called the first developer of the principle of human thought "Minos," with whom the legend of the labyrinth is associated. The fact that human beings can fall into error is symbolized by the labyrinth. Labyrinths were first built at the time when the gods withdrew from human beings. They are, of course, images of the convolutions of the brain, in which the thinker can get lost. At the time of Minos people sensed that they had gradually moved away from being guided directly by the gods and were developing a new form of guidance in which the I experienced the influence of the higher spiritual world.

To summarize: Besides the forerunners of the human race, who completed their human stage on the Moon and have now become angels, there are other beings who did not complete their development at that time. While the angeloi or dhyanic beings advanced one level above ours at the moment when human evolution began on earth, these other beings, like the higher categories of luciferic beings, did not complete their human evolution on the old Moon, and thus remain somehow incomplete.

Thus when the earthly condition of our planet began these early human beings were not alone; they received inspiration from divine-spiritual beings. Without their inspiration, like children without guidance, these early human beings would have been unable to progress. Therefore the beings who had completed their evolution on the old Moon were indirectly present on the earth with them. Between these angelic beings and early, childlike humankind, however, there lived beings who had *not* completed their evolution on the old Moon. These beings, of course, were on a higher level than we are because they could have become angels during the old Moon period. But they had not reached full maturity then and thus remained below the angels, although they are still far superior to us in terms of typically human attributes. Indeed, these beings who stand between us and the angels occupy the lowest level among the multitudes of luciferic spirits — the realm of the luciferic beings begins with them.

It is extraordinarily easy to misunderstand these beings. We could ask why the divine spirits, the rulers of the good, permitted such beings to remain behind, thus allowing the luciferic principle to enter humanity. While we may object that the good gods will certainly turn everything to the good, this question nevertheless suggests itself. Another misunderstanding arises if we consider these beings as simply "evil." To think that these beings are "evil," however, is to misunderstand them because, although they are the source of evil in human evolution, they are not "evil" at all. Rather, they just stand midway between us and the superhuman beings. In a certain way, indeed, these beings are more perfect than we are. They have already achieved a high level of mastery in all the capacities we still have to acquire. At the same time, unlike the angelic forerunners of the human race, these luciferic beings, because they did not complete their human stage of development on the old Moon, are still able to incarnate in human bodies during earthly evolution. The angeloi, on the other hand, the great inspirers of humanity upon whom the ancient Egyptians still relied, cannot appear in human bodies but can only reveal themselves through human beings. Thus, in the remote past, besides human beings and angels, there existed beings who were neither angels nor humans and were able to incarnate in human bodies. Indeed, in Lemurian and Atlantean times a number of individuals bore such "retarded" angelic beings within them as their innermost core. During those periods ordinary human beings, who were to develop through successive incarnations to an appropriate level of the human ideal, coexisted with beings who looked outwardly like ordinary people. These luciferic beings had to clothe themselves in human bodies because earthly conditions require the outward form of a physical body. Thus, particularly in ancient times, humanity lived side by side with these other beings who belong to the lowest category of luciferic individualities.

While the angels worked on human culture through human individuals, the luciferic beings incarnated and founded cultures in various places. The legends of ancient peoples often talk about great persons who established cultures in this or that particular place. These were embodied luciferic beings. However, it would be wrong to assume that because such an individual was an incarnation of a luciferic being he or she was therefore necessarily evil. In fact, human culture has received countless blessings from these beings.

According to spiritual science, in ancient times, specifically in the Atlantean period, there existed a kind of human primal or root language that was the same over all the earth because speech in those times came much more out of the innermost core of the soul than it does today. The following will make this clear. In Atlantean times people experienced outer impressions in such a way that to give expression to something external the soul was compelled to use a *consonant*. Thus, what was present in space — the universe and everything in it — induced people to imitate everything around them with consonants. People felt the wind blowing, the sound of waves, the shelter a house provides, and imitated these experiences by means of consonants. On the other hand, people's inner experiences, such as pain or joy, were imitated by *vowels*. Thus, one can see that in speech the soul became one with external events or beings.

The Akashic chronicle reveals, for example, that when people in the past approached a hut arching over a family, sheltering and protecting the people, they observed primarily its shape curving around the inhabitants.[7] This protective curving of the hut was expressed through a *consonant*, but the fact that there were ensouled bodies in the hut — people could feel this sympathetically — was expressed through a *vowel*. Gradually, the concept of protection emerged: "I have protection, protection for human bodies." This concept was expressed in consonants and vowels, which were not arbitrary, but an unambiguous and direct expression of the experience.

This was the case everywhere on earth. The existence of a "primal language" common to all people is not a figment of the imagination. To a certain extent, the initiates of every nation are still able to understand this original language. Every language contains certain sounds reminiscent of it; in fact, our modern languages are the relics of the primeval, universal human language.

This original language was inspired by the superhuman beings, our true forerunners, who completed their development on the Moon. If there had been no other influence than this, the entire human race would basically have remained unified; there would have been one universal way of speaking and thinking everywhere on earth. Individuality and diversity could not have developed, and human freedom likewise could not have been established. Divisions and splits in humanity were necessary for the development of human individuality. Languages became different in each region of the earth because of the work of those teachers who were an incarnation of a luciferic being. These luciferic or "retarded" angelic beings used the language of the nation in which they incarnated for their teaching. Thus, we owe the fact that every nation speaks a particular, nonuniversal language to the presence of such great, enlightening teachers, who were, in fact, "retarded" angelic beings who had reached a far higher level than the human beings around them. Beings like the early heroes celebrated by the ancient Greeks who worked in human form, for example, as well as beings who worked in human form in other nations, were such incarnations of angelic beings who had not completed their development.

Clearly, then, these beings cannot be dismissed as completely "evil." On the contrary, they have provided what has destined the human race to be free by introducing diversity into what would otherwise have remained universally uniform over the whole earth. This is true for many other aspects of life as well as for languages. Individualization, differentiation, and freedom are due to the beings who remained behind on the Moon.

To be sure, it may be said that the wise leadership of the world intended to guide all beings to their goal in the planetary evolution. However, if this had been done directly, certain other things would not have been achieved. Certain beings are held back in their development because they have a special task in the evolution of humanity. The beings who had completely fulfilled their task on the Moon would have created only a uniform humanity and, therefore, they had to be opposed by the luciferic beings. And this in turn gave these luciferic beings the possibility of changing something that was actually a defect into something good.

On this basis we can consider the question of why evil, imperfection, and disease exist in the world from a wider perspective. We can look at "evil" in exactly the same way we have just looked at the imperfect, "retarded" angelic beings. Everything that is at one time imperfect or retarded in its development is changed into something good in the course of evolution. This is, of course, no justification of our evil deeds.

This also tells us why the wise government of the world holds back the development of certain beings and prevents them from reaching their goal. The reason is that the holding back will serve a good purpose in subsequent evolutionary periods. In ancient times, when the nations were not yet able to direct themselves, teachers guided particular eras and particular individuals. In a sense, all the teachers of the nations—Kadmos, Kekrops, Pelops, Theseus, and so on—bore an angelic being in the innermost depths of their soul.[8] This is a clear indication that humanity is in fact subject to guidance and direction in this respect as well.

Thus, at each stage of evolution there are beings who fail to reach the goal they should have attained. In ancient Egyptian civilization, which flourished several thousand years ago on the banks of the Nile, superhuman teachers revealed themselves to the people and were considered by them to be divine guides. At the same time, however, other beings were active who had not yet completely reached the level of angels.

The ancient Egyptians had attained a certain level of development—that is, the souls of people today had developed to a certain level during the Egyptian period. Thus the guidance I am talking about here has a twofold benefit: it helps the person who is guided to achieve something, and it also helps the guiding beings to advance in their development. For example, an angel is *more* after having guided people for a while than it was before taking this guiding role. In other words, angels advance through their guiding work — "full" angels as well as those who have not yet completed their development. All beings can advance at all times; everything is in continuous development. Nevertheless, at each stage some beings remain behind and fail to complete their development.

Ancient Egyptian culture, therefore, was influenced by three categories of beings: divine leaders or angels, semi-divine leaders who had not yet fully reached the level of angels, and human beings. Now while the human beings on earth progressed in their evolution during the ancient Egyptian period, some superhuman beings or angels were held back, that is, they did not fulfill their guiding role in a way that would have allowed them to bring all of their powers to expression. Consequently, these beings remained behind as angels and did not develop further. Similarly, the imperfect, "retarded" angelic beings, who had not yet developed to the level of the "full" angels, were also arrested in their development. Thus, when the Egypto-Chaldean cultural period drew to a close and the Greco-Latin period began, guiding beings from the earlier cultural epoch who had not finished their development were still present. However, they could now no longer use their powers because their place in guiding humanity had been taken over by other angels or semi-angelic beings. As a result, these beings who were left over, so to speak, were unable to continue their own evolution. Thus we have a category of beings who could have used their powers during the Egyptian period, but did not do so to the full extent possible and so were unable in the subsequent Greco-Latin period to use their own forces because other guiding beings had taken their place. In addition, the nature and character of the Greco-Latin epoch also made their intervention impossible.

Earlier we saw that the beings who had not evolved to the level of angels on the old Moon later had the task of actively participating in the earthly evolution of humanity. By the same token, those guiding beings who did not complete their development in the Egypto-Chaldean period are similarly meant to intervene in human development in a later epoch. This is to say that, in a given later cultural epoch, the normal progress of human evolution is to be directed by beings whose turn it is to take on a guiding role; but, at the same time, other beings will be active who did not develop fully in earlier times, for instance, those who failed to complete their development in the ancient Egyptian epoch. This characterization applies to our own period as well; that is, we live in a time when, besides the normal leaders of humanity, the incompletely developed beings from the ancient Egypto-Chaldean cultural period actively intervene.

To understand the unfolding of events and beings, we must see events in the physical world as effects (revelations) of causes or archetypes that lie in the spiritual world. Our culture, by and large, is characterized by a trend toward spirituality. The urgent striving for spirituality we see in many people is the result of the work of those spiritual guides who have attained the developmental level appropriate to them. These normally developed spiritual

guides of our evolution are at work in everything that can
lead us to the great treasures of spiritual wisdom that theosophy [anthroposophy] can impart to us.

However, the beings who did not develop properly
during the Egypto-Chaldean period are also shaping the
cultural trends of our time. They are at work in much that
is thought and done in the present and the near future. In
particular, these beings are active in everything that gives
our culture a *materialistic* cast, but often their influence
can be felt even in the trend toward the spiritual. Indeed,
we are experiencing what amounts to a resurrection of
Egyptian culture in our time.

The beings invisibly guiding events in the physical
world thus belong to one of two classes. The first com-
prises those spiritual individualities who developed properly and normally up to our time. These were able to help
in the guidance of our culture at the time when the leaders
of the Greco-Latin period preceding our own gradually
completed their mission of guiding humanity through the
first Christian millennium. The second class works together with the first and consists of those spiritual individualities who did not complete their development in the
Egypto-Chaldean period. These had to remain inactive
during the Greco-Latin period, but they can actively participate in guiding us now, because our time is very similar to the Egypto-Chaldean period.

That is why much in contemporary culture seems to be
a resurrection of ancient Egyptian forces. However, the
forces that worked spiritually in ancient Egypt now frequently appear recast in materialistic form. Let us look,

for example, at the way ancient Egyptian knowledge is being revived today. In this connection, we may think of Kepler, who was imbued with a sense of the harmony of the structure of the cosmos and expressed this harmony in the important mathematical laws of celestial mechanics called Kepler's laws.[9] These laws may appear to us now rather dry and abstract, but they grew directly out of Kepler's perception of the harmony of the universe. Kepler himself wrote that to be able to make his discoveries he had to penetrate the holy mysteries of the Egyptians and steal the holy vessels from their temples.[10] What he thus brought the world will not be understood in its full significance for humanity until much later.

Kepler's words are not mere phrases; rather, they indicate that he vaguely sensed that he was reexperiencing what he had learned in Egyptian times during his incarnation in that epoch. Indeed, we can assume that, in a past life, Kepler had deeply studied and penetrated ancient Egyptian wisdom which then reappeared in his soul in a new form appropriate to modern times. Understandably, the Egyptian spirit brings a materialistic trend into our culture since a strong element of materialism existed in Egyptian spirituality. For example, the Egyptians embalmed corpses, that is, they attached great importance to the preservation of the physical body. Our funerary customs, though with appropriate modifications, derive from this Egyptian tradition.

The same forces that failed to develop properly at that time are now again actively participating in human evolution — though, of course, in a different way. The modern worship of mere matter grew out of the outlook that made the embalming of bodies important. The Egyptians embalmed the bodies of their dead and thus preserved something they considered very important. They believed that the further development of the soul after death was linked to the preservation of the physical body. In the same way, modern anatomists dissect the physical body and think that they are learning something about the laws of the human organism.

Today, the forces of the ancient Egyptian and Chaldean worlds that were progressive then have become regressive and are at work in modern science. To fully appreciate the character of our present time, we must come to *know* these forces. If we remain ignorant of their significance, these forces will harm us. Only if we are aware of their activity and can find a right relationship to them will they not be harmful. Only through knowing them will we be able to guide these forces to good ends. They must be put to use, for without them we would not have the great achievements of technology, industry, and so on. These forces belong to the lowest rank of luciferic beings. We must see them for what they are. Otherwise, we begin to believe that no other impulses than the modern materialistic ones exist, and we fail to see other forces that can guide us upward to the spiritual realm. For this reason, we must clearly distinguish two spiritual streams in our time.

If the wise powers guiding the world had not retarded the development of these luciferic beings during the Egypto-Chaldean period, our era would lack a certain necessary gravity. Only the forces that would bring us at all costs into the spiritual realm would then be working on us. Of course, we would be only too inclined to give in to them and would become dreamers and visionaries; we would be interested in life only if it became spiritualized as quickly as possible. A certain contempt for the physical-material world would then be our typical attitude. However, to fulfill its mission, our present cultural epoch has to bring the forces of the material world fully to fruition, so that their sphere can be conquered for spirituality.

We can be tempted and seduced by the most beautiful things if we pursue them one-sidedly, and this one-sidedness, if it takes hold, can also turn every good endeavor and striving into fanaticism. It is true that humanity advances through its noble impulses, but it is also true that the impassioned and fanatic advocacy of the noblest impulses can bring about the worst results for our development. Only when we strive toward the highest goals with humility and clarity, and not out of impassioned enthusiasm, will wholesome and healthy developments for the progress of humanity result.

Therefore, the wisdom at work in guiding the world arrested the development of those forces that should have fully evolved during the Egyptian cultural epoch. This was done to give the achievements of our era a certain necessary weight, thereby enabling us to understand the material world, the things on the physical plane. These same forces now direct our attention toward physical life.

Thus, humanity develops under the guidance of beings that have progressed properly and of other beings that failed to do so. People with clairvoyant vision can observe the cooperation of the two classes of beings in the supersensible world. They can understand the spiritual processes of which the physical events around us are the manifestation.

Of course, opening our spiritual eye or spiritual ear to the spiritual world through exercises of some kind is not sufficient to enable us to understand what is happening in the world process. It only allows us to *see* what is there, to recognize that there are spiritual beings of the soul or the spiritual realm. In addition to this, we must also be able to distinguish, to cognize the different kinds of spiritual beings involved in the world process. We cannot tell just by looking whether a being of the soul or spiritual realm is developing appropriately or whether its development has been arrested. We do not know whether it advances or hinders our evolution. If we develop clairvoyant abilities but do not also gain a full understanding of the conditions of human development as we have described them, we will never be able to tell what type of being we are encountering. Thus, clairvoyance must always be accompanied by a clear assessment of what we perceive in the supersensible world.

This is particularly necessary in our own time. It was not always so. In very ancient cultures, things were quite different. In ancient Egypt, for example, clairvoyants could identify to what group a being of the supersensible world belonged, because that information was as if written on its forehead. Therefore, clairvoyants could not mistake one being for another. Nowadays, however, the danger of misunderstanding and mistaking one being for another is very great. In ancient times, people were still close to the realm of the spiritual hierarchies and could recognize the beings they encountered. Now, however, errors are easily possible, and the only way to protect ourselves against serious harm is to make an effort to grasp concepts and ideas such as those presented here.

In esotericism, a person who is able to see into the spiritual world is called a "clairvoyant." But, as I have said, just being a clairvoyant is not enough, because clairvoyants, though they can see in the supersensible world, cannot distinguish. Therefore, people who have developed the ability to distinguish between the beings and events of the higher worlds are called *"initiates."* Initiation is what enables us to distinguish between various types of beings. People can be clairvoyant and see into the higher worlds without also being initiates. In ancient times, being able to distinguish between these beings was not especially important, for once the ancient mystery schools had brought their students to the point of clairvoyance, there was no great danger of making mistakes. Now, however, the danger of falling into error is very great. Therefore, in all esoteric schooling the development of clairvoyance must always be accompanied by initiation. As people become clairvoyant, they must also become able to distinguish between the particular types of supersensible beings and occurrences they perceive.

In modern times, the powers guiding humanity are faced with the special task of creating a balance between the principles of clairvoyance and initiation. At the beginning of the modern period, the leading spiritual teachers necessarily had to consider what I have just explained. As a matter of principle, therefore, the esoteric spiritual movement that is suited to our time works to establish the right relationship between clairvoyance and initiation. This balanced relationship became necessary when, in the thirteenth century, humanity underwent a crisis in regard to its faculty of higher cognition. Around the year 1250, in fact, we find the period in which people felt most cut off from the spiritual world.

Clairvoyant exploration of this time reveals that even the outstanding minds striving for higher cognition had to admit that their ability to know the physical world was limited by their reason, intellect, and spiritual knowledge. They felt that human research and the human capacity to know would never enable them to reach the spiritual world. In fact, they only knew of the existence of a spiritual world because reports of it had been handed down from previous generations. In the thirteenth century, then, direct spiritual perception of the higher worlds had become darkened and more difficult. It was with good reason, therefore, that at the height of scholasticism people believed that human knowledge was restricted to the physical world.[11]

By about 1250, people had to draw the boundary between what they believed on the basis of the traditions handed down to them and what they could perceive and understand on their own. The latter was limited to the physical, sensory world. Later, a new era dawned when it began to be possible again to gain direct insight into the spiritual world. However, this new clairvoyance is different from the old one that had more or less disappeared by the year 1250.

For this new form of clairvoyance, Western esotericism had to lay down the strict principle that *initiation* must always guide our spiritual ears and eyes. This characterizes the special task that the esoteric stream, then introduced into Europe, had taken upon itself. As the year 1250 approached, a new way of guiding human beings toward the supersensible worlds began to take hold.

This new guidance was prepared by the spirits that worked in that time behind the outer events of history. Already centuries earlier, they had prepared what would be necessary for esoteric schooling under the conditions that would prevail after 1250. If the term "modern esotericism" is not a misnomer, we can apply it to the spiritual work of these more highly developed individuals. Conventional history, focusing only on outer events, knows nothing of them. But their deeds have affected all cultural developments in the West since the thirteenth century.

The significance of the year 1250 for the spiritual development of humanity becomes especially clear if we consider the following result of clairvoyant research. Even individualities who had already reached high levels of spiritual development in their previous incarnations and incarnated again around 1250 had to experience a complete, though temporary, obscuring of their direct vision of the spiritual world. Even completely enlightened individuals were as though cut off from the spiritual world and knew about it only from their memories of earlier incarnations. From this we can see that a new element obviously had to appear in the spiritual guidance of humanity. This new element is true modern esotericism. It enables us to fully understand how what we call the Christ-impulse can take part in guiding humanity as well as each individual in all activities and aspects of life.

The Christ-principle was first assimilated by human souls in the period between the Mystery of Golgotha and the advent of modern esotericism. During this period, people accepted Christ unconsciously as far as their higher spiritual forces were concerned. Later, when people had to accept Christ consciously, they made all sorts of mistakes. In their understanding of Christ they were led into a labyrinth. In those first years of Christianity, the Christ-principle took root in lower, subordinate soul forces. This was followed by a time, one in which we are still living, in which people began to understand the Christ-principle with their higher soul capacities. In fact, even today, we are only at the beginning of this understanding. Indeed, as I will explain in the next chapter, the decline of supersensible cognition up to the thirteenth century and its slow revival in a new and different form since then coincide with the intervention of the Christ-impulse in human history. Modern esotericism, therefore, may be understood as the elevation of the Christ-impulse into the leading element in the guidance of those souls who want to work on gaining a knowledge of the higher worlds that is appropriate to current developmental conditions.

LECTURE THREE

AS I EXPLAINED in my preceding remarks, it is the beings who completed their human stage of development during the previous incarnation of the earth — the old moon period — who guide human spiritual evolution. Their guidance, however, is obstructed and opposed by beings who did not complete their development during the moon period. Nevertheless, while these "imperfect" beings obstruct the guiding activity of those who completed their development, they also, paradoxically, further it. The resistance they offer to our progress strengthens, solidifies, and lends increased weight and significance to the forces that are called forth by the beings who advance our development. In Christian esotericism, these classes of superhuman beings who have attained the developmental level immediately above our own, both those who advance our development and those who help us by introducing obstacles, are called angels or angeloi. Above them are the beings of the higher hierarchies, the arch-angels, archai, and so on, who also take part in guiding humanity.

In each of these hierarchies we find beings of varying degrees of perfection. At the beginning of the present earth's evolution, for instance, we find angeloi of higher and lower standing. Those of higher standing barely attained the minimum level of development when the moon stage of evolution ended and the earth stage began, while those of higher standing had passed far beyond it. Between these two types are to be found angeloi of every possible level of development whose participation in the guidance of human evolution on earth is in accordance with the level they have attained. Thus, the beings who had the guiding role in Egyptian cultural development were those who had reached a higher stage of perfection on the Moon than those who guided humanity during the Greco-Latin age, and these, in turn, were more perfect than the beings who guide us now. Those who were to guide humanity later trained themselves for this task during the Egyptian and the Greek periods. By this means, they were prepared to guide a culture that had progressed further.

In the time period following the Atlantean catastrophe seven successive cultural epochs may be distinguished: first, the ancient Indian; second, the ancient Persian;* third, the Egypto-Chaldean; and fourth, the Greco-Latin. Our own period, which began around the twelfth century, constitutes the fifth cultural epoch and, although we are

---

*Ancient Persian here does not refer to what is called "Persian" in ordinary history but rather to an ancient Asian prehistoric (Iranian) culture that developed in the region where the Persian Empire flourished later.

still in the middle of it, the first preparations for the sixth epoch are already underway. In other words, these individual periods of evolution overlap and transitions are very gradual. A seventh post-Atlantean epoch will follow the sixth.

Looking more closely at the guidance of humanity, we realize that it was only in the third cultural epoch — the Egypto-Chaldean — that the angels or lower dhyanic beings became to some extent independent guides of human evolution. This was not the case in the ancient Persian period. The angels then did not yet possess this independence and were subordinate to a higher guidance to a greater degree than they were during the Egyptian period. In ancient Persian times, angels still worked according to the impulses of the hierarchy above them. Thus, although everything was already subject to the angels' guidance, they themselves submitted to the direction of the archangels (archangeloi).

In the age of ancient India, on the other hand, during which post-Atlantean life reached unequaled spiritual heights — natural heights — under the guidance of great human teachers, the archangels themselves were still subject to a higher guidance, namely, that of the archai or "primal beginnings."

Thus we may say that from the Indian period on, through the ancient Persian and Egypto-Chaldean cultures, certain beings of the higher hierarchies increasingly withdrew from the direct guidance of humanity. Consequently, by the time of the fourth, Greco-Latin post-Atlantean cultural period, human beings had become, in certain respects, entirely independent. To be sure, the superhuman beings described above still guided human evolution, but they held the reins as loosely as possible.

As a result, the spiritual beings guiding humanity benefited as much from our actions as we did ourselves. This explains the entirely "human" character of the Greco-Roman period: human beings were left completely to their own resources. The characteristics of art and political life in the Greek and Roman epochs grew out of this necessity of human beings to live out their individuality in their own way.

When we consider very early periods of cultural history, we find humanity guided by beings who had reached their human level of development in earlier planetary stages. The fourth, Greco-Latin epoch was intended to test human beings to the greatest extent possible. For this reason, the entire spiritual leadership of humanity had to be arranged in a new way.

In our epoch, the fifth post-Atlantean one, the beings guiding us belong to the same hierarchy that ruled the ancient Egyptians and Chaldeans. The beings who were guiding people then are in fact now resuming their activities. As I said above, certain of these beings remained behind in their development, and we can feel their influence now in today's materialistic feelings and perceptions.

Both the angelic (or lower dhyanic) beings that advance our development, as well as those who try to obstruct it, progressed in their development by guiding the ancient Egyptians and Chaldeans through qualities they had themselves acquired in very ancient times. At the

same time, through their work of guidance they advanced
their own development. Thus, these advancing angeloi
are guiding our fifth post-Atlantean epoch with abilities
they acquired during the Egypto-Chaldean period. As a
result of this progress, they can now develop very special
capabilities. Namely, they have qualified themselves to
be filled with forces that flow from the most important
being of the whole of earthly evolution. The power of
Christ works on them.

This power works not only in the physical world
through Jesus of Nazareth but also in the spiritual worlds
on superhuman beings. Christ exists not only for the earth
but also for these higher beings. The beings who guided
ancient Egypto-Chaldean culture were not then guided by
Christ; they submitted to Christ's guidance only later.
This submission was the step in their development that
enabled them to guide the fifth post-Atlantean period
under Christ's influence. Now they are followers of Christ
in the higher worlds.

On the other hand, the angelic beings I have described
as obstructing our development were held back in their
development precisely because they did not submit to
Christ's leadership and continue to work independently.
This is why the materialistic trend in our culture will become more and more pronounced. There will be a materialistic stream guided by the Egypto-Chaldean spirits
whose development was held back. Most of what is called
modern materialistic science is under this influence.

Besides this influence, a second, different stream is
also making itself felt. This is geared to helping us find

the Christ-principle, as we call it, in all we do. For example, some people today claim that our world consists, in the final analysis, only of atoms. Who instills into human beings the idea that the world consists only of atoms? They get this idea from the superhuman angelic beings whose development was arrested during the Egypto-Chaldean period. However, the angelic beings who reached their goal in the ancient Egypto-Chaldean cultural period and encountered Christ at that time can instill other ideas in us. They can teach us that substance is permeated with the spirit of Christ right down to the smallest parts of the world. And, however strange it may seem now, a time will come when chemistry and physics will not be taught as they are today under the influence of the Egypto-Chaldean spirits whose development was held back. Instead, scientists will teach that matter is built up piece by piece the way *Christ* ordered it. People will find Christ even in the laws of chemistry and physics, and a spiritual chemistry and a spiritual physics will develop.

Undoubtedly this now seems to many people merely a daydream or worse. But yesterday's folly is often tomorrow's wisdom. Careful observers can already discern the factors working toward this end in our cultural development. At the same time, of course, such observers know only too well the scientific or philosophical objections that can be raised — with apparent justification — against this supposed folly.

On the basis of the assumptions presented here, we can understand the advantages the guiding superhuman

beings have over us. Post-Atlantean humanity encountered Christ when the Christ-event entered human history
in the fourth post-Atlantean or Greco-Latin epoch. The
superhuman guiding beings encountered Christ during
the Egypto-Chaldean period and worked their way up toward him. Then, during the Greco-Latin epoch, they had
to leave humanity to its fate, in order later to take part in
guiding its development again. Today when we practice
theosophy [anthroposophy] this means that we acknowledge that the superhuman beings who guided humanity in
the past are now continuing their guiding function by sub-
mitting themselves to Christ's leadership. The same is
also true for other beings.

In the ancient Persian epoch archangels took part in
guiding humanity. They submitted to the leadership of
Christ even earlier than the beings of the lower hierarchies. Zarathustra, for example, turned the attention of his
followers and his people to the sun, telling them that the
great spirit Ahura Mazda, "he who will come down to
earth," lives in the sun.[1] The archangels who guided Zarathustra taught him about the great sun-guide who had not
yet come down to earth but had only started on his way so
as to later be able to intervene *directly* in earthly evolution. Similarly, the guiding beings presiding over the
great teachers of India taught them about the Christ of the
future. It is an error to think that these teachers knew
nothing about Christ. They only said he was "above their
sphere," and that they "could not reach him."

As in our fifth cultural epoch it is the angels who
bring Christ into our spiritual development, so in the

sixth cultural epoch we will be guided by the beings who
guided the ancient Persian epoch. The spirits of primal
beginning, the archai, who guided humanity in ancient
India, will, under Christ, guide humanity in the seventh
cultural epoch. In Greco-Latin times, Christ came down
from spiritual heights and revealed himself in the flesh in
the body of Jesus of Nazareth — he descended right into
the physical world. When they are ready, human beings
will find Christ again in the next higher world. In the future, Christ will no longer be found in the physical world
but only in the worlds directly above it.

After all, human beings will not always remain as they
are now. We will become more mature and will find
Christ in the spiritual world, as Paul did in the event on
the road to Damascus, an event that prophetically fore-
shadows the future. And as the great teachers who led humanity in the Egypto-Chaldean epoch also guide us, so
too it will be they who will lead us in the twentieth century to a vision of Christ similar to the one Paul saw. They
will show us that Christ works not only on the earth but
spiritualizes the entire solar system. Then, in the seventh
cultural epoch, the reincarnated holy teachers of India
will proclaim Christ as the great spirit, whose presence
they first sensed in the unity of Brahman but which received its meaning and content only through Christ.[2]
They will recognize Christ as the spirit they believed to
rule above their sphere. Thus, step by step, humanity is
led into the spiritual world.

To speak of Christ as the leader of successive worlds
and of the higher hierarchies is the teaching of the science

that has unfolded since the twelfth and thirteenth centuries under the sign of the Rose Cross, a science that has increasingly proven essential for humanity.[3] Looking at Christ from this perspective, we gain new insights into the being who lived in Palestine and then fulfilled the Mystery of Golgotha, as the following shows.

There have been many different views of Christ before today's. For example, certain Christian gnostics of the first centuries claimed that the Christ who lived in Palestine did not have a physical body of flesh at all but had only an apparent — etheric — body that became visible to physical eyes.[4] Consequently, since for them only an etheric body was present, they said Christ's death on the cross was not a real death but only an apparent one. There were also various disputes among the adherents of Christianity — for example, the famous dispute between the Arians and the Athanasians,[5] and so on — as well as many different interpretations of the true nature of Christ. Many different views of Christ, indeed, have been held by people right into our own time.

Spiritual science, however, must see Christ not just as an earthly being but as a *cosmic* being. In a certain sense, we human beings are also cosmic beings. We live a dual life: a physical life in the physical body from birth until death and a life in the spiritual worlds between death and rebirth. While we are incarnated in the physical body, we are dependent on the earth because the physical body is subject to the living conditions and forces of the earth. We ingest the substances and forces of the earth, and we are also part of the earth's physical organism. But once we have passed through the portal of death, we no longer belong to the forces of the earth.

Yet, it would be wrong to imagine that having passed through the portal of death we do not belong to any forces at all, for after death we are connected with the forces of the solar system and the other galaxies. Between death and rebirth we live in and belong to the cosmos in the same way as between birth and death we live in the earthly realm and belong to the elements of air, water, earth and so on. After death, we enter the realm of cosmic influences; for example, the planets affect us not only with gravity and other physical forces explained by physical astronomy but also with their spiritual forces. Indeed, we are connected with these cosmic spiritual forces after death, each of us in a particular way appropriate to our individuality. Just as a person born in Europe has a different relationship to temperature conditions and so on than a person born in Australia, so each of us similarly has a unique, individual relationship to the forces working on us during life after death. One person may have a closer relationship to the forces of Mars while another is more closely connected to those of Jupiter and yet others may have a closer relationship to the forces of the entire galaxy, and so on. These forces also lead us back to the earth to our new life. Thus, before our rebirth we are connected with the entire starry universe.

The unique relationship of an individual to the cosmic system determines which forces lead him or her back to earth; they also determine to which parents and to which locality we are brought. The impulse to incarnate in one place or another, in this or that family, in this or that nation, at this or that point in time, is determined by the way the individual is integrated into the cosmos before birth.

In the past the German language had an expression that poignantly characterized the birth of an individual. When someone was born, people said that he or she had "become young" (*"ist jung geworden"*). Unconsciously, this expression indicates that following death we are first subject to the forces that made us old in our previous incarnation, but just before our new birth, these are replaced by other forces that make us "young" again. In his drama *Faust*, Goethe says of someone that he "became young in *Nebelland* (the land of mist)"; *Nebelland* is the old name for medieval Germany.[6]

People who are knowledgeable about these things can "read" the forces that determine a person's path in his or her physical life; on this basis horoscopes are cast. Each of us is assigned a particular horoscope, in which the forces are revealed that have led us into this life. For example, if in a particular horoscope Mars is above Aries, this means that certain Aries forces cannot pass through Mars but are weakened instead.

Thus, human beings on their way into physical existence can get their bearings through their horoscope. Before ending this discussion — which, after all, seems a daring one in our time — we should note that most of what is presented today in this area is the purest dilettantism and pure superstition. As far as the world at large is concerned, the true science of these things has largely been lost. Therefore, the principles presented here should not be judged according to the claims of modern astrology, which is highly questionable.

The active forces of the starry world push us into physical incarnation. Clairvoyant perception allows us to see in a person's organization that he or she is indeed the result of the working together of such cosmic forces. I want to illustrate this in a hypothetical form that nevertheless corresponds fully to clairvoyant perceptions.

If we examined the structure of a person's brain clairvoyantly and could see that certain functions are located in certain places and give rise to certain processes, we would find that each person's brain is different. No two people have the same brain. If we could take a picture of the entire brain with all of its details visible, we would get a different picture for each person. If we photographed a person's brain at the moment of birth and took a picture of the sky directly above his or her birthplace, the two pictures would be alike. The stars in the photograph of the sky would be arranged in the same way as certain parts of the brain in the other picture. Thus, our brain is really a picture of the heavens, and we each have a different picture depending on where and when we were born. This indicates that we are born out of the entire universe.

This insight gives us an idea of the way the macrocosm manifests in the individual and from this, in turn, we can understand how it manifests in Christ. If we were to think that *after* the Baptism, the macrocosm lived in Christ in the *same* way as it does in any other human being, we would have the wrong idea.

Let us consider for a moment Jesus of Nazareth and his extraordinary life. At the beginning of the Christian era, *two* boys named Jesus were born. One belonged to the Nathan line of the house of David, the other to the Solomon line of the same house. These two boys were born at approximately — though not exactly — the same time.[7]

In the Solomon child portrayed in the Gospel of St. Matthew, the individuality who had lived earlier as Zarathustra incarnated. Thus, in the Jesus depicted in the Gospel of St. Matthew, we actually encounter the reincarnated Zarathustra or Zoroaster.[8] The individuality of Zarathustra grew up in this child just as Matthew describes it, until the boy's twelfth year. Then Zarathustra left his body and entered the body of the other Jesus, the one described by the Gospel of St. Luke. That is why at this moment the child Jesus so suddenly became entirely different from what he had previously been. When his parents found him in the temple in Jerusalem after the spirit of Zarathustra had entered him, they were astonished. This is shown by the fact that they could not understand what he said when they found him for they knew only the Nathan Jesus as he had been before. The Jesus who now stood before them could talk as he did to the scribes in the temple because the spirit of Zarathustra had now entered into him.

The spirit of Zarathustra lived and matured to a still higher perfection in this Jesus, who came from the Nathan line of the house of David, up to his thirtieth year. It should also be noted that impulses from the *Buddha* streamed out of the spiritual world into the *astral* body of this youth, in whom the spirit of Zarathustra now lived.

It is true, as the Eastern tradition teaches, that the Buddha was born as a "bodhisattva" and only reached the rank of buddha on earth in his twenty-ninth year.[9] When Gautama Buddha was still a small child, Asita, the great Indian sage, came weeping to the royal palace. As a seer, Asita knew this royal child would become the "Buddha." He only regretted that, since he was already an old man, he would not live to see the son of Suddhodana become Buddha. This wise man Asita was reborn in the time of Jesus of Nazareth; it is he who is introduced in St. Luke's Gospel as the temple priest and sees the Buddha reveal himself in the Nathan Jesus. And because he saw this he said: "Lord, now lettest thou thy servant depart in peace . . .for mine eyes have seen thy salvation" (Luke 2:29-30). Through the astral body of this Jesus boy — the one presented in the Gospel of St. Luke — Asita could see what he had not been able to see in India: the bodhisattva who has become Buddha.[10]

All of this was necessary for the development of the body that was to receive the Baptism by John in the river Jordan. At the moment of the Baptism, the individuality of Zarathustra left behind the threefold body — physical, etheric, and astral — of the Jesus who had grown up in the complicated way that enabled Zarathustra's spirit to dwell in him — for the reborn Zarathustra had had to undergo the two developmental possibilities represented in the two Jesus boys. Thus John the Baptist was brought before the body of Jesus of Nazareth in whom the cosmic individuality of Christ was now working. Other human beings are placed into their earthly existence through cosmic-spiritual laws, but these are then counteracted by those originating in the conditions of the earth's evolution. In the case of Christ Jesus, however, the cosmic-spiritual powers alone remained active in him after the Baptism. The laws of the earth's evolution did not influence him at all.

During the time that Jesus of Nazareth pursued his ministry and journeys as Jesus Christ in Palestine in the last three years of his life — from the age of thirty to thirty-three — the entire cosmic Christ-being continued to work in him. In other words, Christ always stood under the influence of the entire cosmos; he did not take a single step without cosmic forces working in him. The events of these three years in Jesus' life were a continuous realization of his horoscope, for in every moment during those years there occurred what usually happens only at birth. This was possible because the entire body of the Nathan Jesus had remained susceptible to the influence of the totality of the forces of the cosmic-spiritual hierarchies that guide our earth.

Now that we know that the whole spirit of the cosmos penetrated Christ Jesus we may ask, Who was the being who went to Capernaum and all the other places Jesus went? The being who walked the earth in those years certainly looked like any other human being. But the forces working in him were the cosmic forces coming from the sun and the stars; they directed his body. The total essence of the cosmos, to which the earth belongs, determined what Christ Jesus did. This is why the constellations are so often alluded to in the gospel descriptions of Jesus' activities. For example, in the Gospel of St. John the time when Christ finds his first disciple is described as "about the tenth hour" (John 1:39). In this fact the spirit of the entire cosmos expressed itself in a way appropriate to the appointed moment. Such indications are less obvious in other places in the gospels, but people who can read the gospels properly will find them everywhere.

The miracles of healing the sick must also be under-stood from this point of view. Let us look at just one pas-sage, the one that reads, "Now when the sun was setting, all those who had any that were sick with various diseases brought them to him; and he laid his hands on them and healed them" (Luke 5:40). What does this mean? Here the gospel writer points out that this healing was connected with the constellation of the stars, that in those days the necessary constellation was present only after the sun had set. In other words, in those times the healing forces could manifest themselves only after sunset. Christ Jesus is por-trayed as the mediator who brings together the sick and the forces of the cosmos that could heal them at precisely that time. These were the same forces that also worked as Christ in Jesus. The healing occurred through Christ's presence, which exposed the sick to the healing cosmic forces. These healing forces could be effective only under the appropriate conditions of space and time, as described above. In other words, the forces of the cosmos worked on the sick through their representative, the Christ.

However, these forces could work in this way only while Christ was on earth. Only then were the cosmic constellations so connected to the forces in the human organism that certain diseases could be cured when these constellations worked on individuals through Christ Jesus. A repetition of these conditions in cosmic and earthly evolution is just as impossible as a second incarnation of the Christ in a human body. Thus, the life of Christ Jesus was the earthly expression of a particular relationship between the cosmos and human forces. When sick people remained for a while by Christ's side, their nearness to Christ brought them into a relationship to the macrocosm and this had a healing effect on them.

* * *

What I have said so far allows us to understand how the guidance of humanity has been placed under the influence of Christ. Nevertheless, the other forces whose development was held back in the Egypto-Chaldean epoch also continue to work alongside those that are Christ-filled, as we can see in many contemporary interpretations of the gospels. Books are published that take great pains to show that the gospels can be understood astrologically. The greatest opponents of the gospels cite this astrological interpretation, claiming, for example, that the path of the archangel Gabriel from Elizabeth to Mary represents the movement of the sun from the constellation of Virgo to another one.

To a certain extent, this astrological interpretation is correct; however, in our time, ideas of this sort are instilled into people by the beings whose development was arrested during the Egypto-Chaldean epoch. Under their influence there are some who would have us believe that the gospels are merely allegories representing certain cosmic relationships. The truth is, however, that the whole cosmos is expressed in Christ. In other words, we can characterize Christ's life by describing for each of its events the cosmic relationships that, *through Christ*, entered life on earth.

As soon as we understand all this correctly, we will inevitably and fully accept that Christ lived on earth. The false view mentioned above, however, claims that, because Christ's life is expressed in the gospels through cosmic constellations, it follows necessarily that the gospels are only an allegory of these constellations and that Christ did not really live on earth.

Allow me to use a comparison to make things clear. Imagine every person at birth as a spherical mirror reflecting everything around it. Were we to trace the outlines of the images in the mirror with a pencil, we could then take the mirror and carry the picture it represents with us wherever we went. Just so, we carry a picture of the cosmos within us when we are born, and this *one* picture affects and influences us throughout our lives. Of course, we could also leave the mirror clean as it was originally, in which case it would reflect its surroundings wherever we took it, providing us with a complete picture of the world around us. This analogy explains how Christ was in the time between the Baptism in the Jordan and the Mystery of Golgotha. What enters our earthly life *only* at our birth flowed into Christ Jesus at *each moment* of his life. After the Mystery of Golgotha, what had streamed into Christ from the cosmos merged with the spiritual substance of the earth, and it has been united with the spirit of the earth ever since.

When Paul became clairvoyant on his way to Damascus, he was able to perceive that what had previously been in the cosmos had merged with the spirit of the earth. People who can relive this event in their soul can see this for themselves. In the twentieth century, human beings are able for the first time to experience the Christ-event spiritually, as St. Paul did. Up to this century only those individuals who had gained clairvoyant powers through esoteric schooling were able to have such experiences. Today and in the future, however, as a result of natural human development, advancing soul forces will be able to see Christ in the spiritual sphere of the earth. Beginning with a certain point in the twentieth century, a few people will be able to have such experiences and will be able to relive the incident at Damascus, but thereafter gradually more and more people will be able to do so, and in the distant future it will have become a natural capacity of the human soul to see Christ in this way.

* * *

When Christ entered earthly history, a completely new element was introduced into it. Even the outer events of history bear witness to this. In the first cultural periods after the Atlantean catastrophe, people knew very well that the physical planets, such as Mars, Jupiter, or Saturn, were the expressions or manifestations of spiritual beings.

In later ages this view was completely forgotten. People came to see the heavenly bodies as merely material things — to be judged according to their physical conditions. By the Middle Ages, people saw in the stars only what their physical eyes could perceive: the sphere of Venus, the sphere of the sun, of Mars, and so on up to the sphere of the firmament of fixed stars. Beyond that, they believed, there was the eighth sphere which enclosed the others like a solid blue wall around them.

Then Copernicus came and shook to its foundations the established outlook of relying completely and exclusively on what the human senses could perceive.[11] According to modern natural science, only people with muddled minds can claim that the world is maya or illusion and that we must look into a spiritual world to see the truth. Scientists believe that true science is based on what our senses tell us, and they record those perceptions. However, the only time when astronomers relied exclusively on their senses was in the days when the astronomy prevailed that modern astronomers oppose!

Modern astronomy began to develop as a science when Copernicus started to think about what exists in the universe beyond the range of human sensory perception. In fact, it is true of all the sciences that they developed *in opposition* to sensory appearance. When Copernicus explained that what we see is maya, illusion, and that we should rely on what we *cannot* see — that was the moment when science as we know it today began.

In other words, the modern sciences did not become "science" until they stopped relying exclusively on sensory

perception. Giordano Bruno, as the philosophical interpret-
er of Copernicus's teachings, proclaimed that the eighth
sphere, which had been considered the boundary of space
enclosing everything, was not a boundary at all.[12] It was
maya, an illusion, and only appeared to be the boundary. In
reality, a vast number of worlds had been poured into the
universe. Thus what had previously been regarded as the
boundary of the universe now became the boundary of the
world of human sensory perception. We have to look *beyond* the sense world. Once we no longer see the world
merely as it appears to our senses, then we can perceive
infinity.

Originally, then, humanity had a spiritual view of the
cosmos, but in the course of history this was gradually
lost. The spiritual world view was replaced by an understanding of the world based exclusively on sensory perception. Then the Christ impulse entered human history.
Through this principle humanity was led once again to imbue the materialistic outlook with spirituality. At the moment when Giordano Bruno burst the confines of sensory
appearance, the Christ-development had so far advanced
in him that the soul force, which had been kindled by the
Christ-impulse, could be active within him. This indicates
the significance of Christ's involvement in human history
and development, which is really still in its early stages.

What, then, are the goals of spiritual science?

Spiritual science completes what Bruno and others did
for the outer physical sciences by demonstrating that the
conventional, sense-based sciences can perceive and understand only maya or illusion. At one time, people

looked up to the "eighth sphere" and believed it to be the boundary of the universe. Similarly, modern thinking considers human life bounded by birth and death. Spiritual science extends our view beyond these boundaries.

Ideas like this one allow us to see human evolution as an uninterrupted chain. And, indeed, what Copernicus and Bruno accomplished for space by overcoming sensory appearance had already been known earlier from the inspirations of the spiritual stream that is continued today by spiritual science or theosophy [anthroposophy]. Modern esotericism, as we may call it, worked in a secret and mysterious way on Copernicus, Bruno, Kepler, and others.[13] Thus, people whose outlook is based on the findings of Bruno and Copernicus betray their own traditions when they refuse to accept theosophy [anthroposophy] and insist on looking only at sensory appearance.

Just as Giordano Bruno broke through the blue vault of heaven, so spiritual science breaks through the boundaries of birth and death and proves that the human being comes forth from the macrocosm to live in this physical life and returns again to a macrocosmic existence after death. What is revealed in the individual on a limited scale can be seen on a much larger scale in the representative of the cosmic spirit, in Christ Jesus. The impulse Christ gave to evolution could be given only *once*. Only once could the entire cosmos be reflected as it was in Christ; the constellation that existed then will not appear again. This constellation had to work through a human body in order to be able to impart its impulse to the earth. Just as this particular constellation will not occur a second time, so

Christ will not incarnate again. People claim that Christ will appear again on earth only because they do not know that Christ is the representative of the entire universe and because they cannot find the way to the Christ-idea presented in all its elements by spiritual science.

Thus, modern spiritual science or theosophy [anthroposophy] has developed a Christ-idea that shows us our kinship with the entire macrocosm in a new way. To really know Christ we need the inspiring forces that are now imparted through the ancient Egyptian and Chaldean superhuman beings who were themselves guided by Christ. We need this *new* inspiration, which has been prepared by the great esotericists of the Middle Ages since the thirteenth century. This new inspiration must now be brought more and more to the attention of the general public. If we prepare the soul properly for the perception of the spiritual world according to the teachings of spiritual science, we will be able to hear clairaudiently and to see clairvoyantly what is revealed by these ancient Chaldean and Egyptian powers, who have now become spiritual guides under the leadership of the Christ-being. The first Christian centuries up to our own time were only the preparation for what humanity will receive and understand one day.

In the future, people's hearts will be filled with a Christ-idea whose magnitude will surpass anything humanity has known and understood so far. The first impulse that Christ brought and the understanding of him that has lived on until now is even in the best exponents of the Christ-principle only a preparation for a true understanding of Christ. Strangely enough, those who present the Christ-idea in this way in the West will in all probability be accused of not basing themselves on western Christian tradition. After all, this western Christian tradition is utterly inadequate for understanding Christ in the near future.

Western esotericism allows us to see the spiritual guidance of humanity gradually merge with the guidance proceeding from the Christ-impulse. Modern esotericism will gradually flow into people's hearts, and the spiritual guidance of the individual and humanity will more and more be seen consciously in this light.

Let us recall that the Christ-principle first entered human hearts when Christ ministered in Palestine in the physical body of Jesus of Nazareth. In those days, people who had gradually resigned themselves to trusting only in the sensory world could receive the impulse appropriate to their understanding. The same impulse then worked through modern esotericism to inspire such great minds as Nicholas of Cusa, Copernicus, and Galileo.[14] That is why Copernicus could assert that sensory appearance cannot teach us the truth about the solar system and that we must look beyond it to find the truth.

At that time, people were not yet mature enough — even a brilliant man like Giordano Bruno was not yet ready — to integrate themselves *consciously* into the stream of modern esotericism. The spirit of this stream had to work in them without their being conscious of it. Giordano Bruno proclaimed proudly that the human being is actually a macrocosmic being condensed into a monad to enter physical existence; and that this monad expands again when the individual dies. What had been condensed in the body expands into the universe in order to concentrate again at other levels of existence and to expand again, and so on. Bruno expressed great concepts that fully agree with modern esotericism, even though they may sound like stammering to our modern ears.

We are not necessarily always conscious of the spiritual influences that guide us. For example, such influences led Galileo into the cathedral of Pisa. Thousands of people had seen the old church lamp there, but they did not look at it the way he did. Galileo saw the lamp swing and compared its oscillations with his pulse beats. In this way he discovered that the church lamp swung in a regular rhythm similar to that of his pulse — the "law of the pendulum," as it is known in modern physics. Anyone familiar with modern physics knows that physics as we know it would not exist if it had not been for Galileo's laws. What was at work in leading Galileo to the swinging lamp in the cathedral — thus giving modern physics its first principles — now works in spiritual science. The powers that guide us spiritually work secretly in this way.

We are now approaching a time when we have to become conscious of these guiding powers. We will be able to understand better what must happen in the future if we correctly grasp the inspiration coming to us from modern esotericism. From this inspiration we also know that the spiritual beings whom the ancient Egyptians considered to be their teachers — the same beings who ruled as gods — are ruling again, but that they now want to submit to Christ's leadership. People will feel more and more that they can allow pre-Christian elements to be resurrected in glory and style on a higher level. In the present era we need a strengthened consciousness, a high sense of duty and responsibility concerning the understanding of the spiritual world. For this to enter our soul we must understand the mission of spiritual science in the way I have outlined.

APPENDIX

Introductory Comments to the Lecture Cycle
The Spiritual Guidance of the Individual and Humanity
Copenhagen, June 5, 1911

The Mission of the New Revelation of the Spirit

In the next few days I will have the opportunity to speak
here about a theosophical subject that is important to me,
namely, the spiritual guidance of the individual and humanity. Since our friends here have asked me to, I will
preface my lecture series today with a few comments that
may serve as a kind of introduction to the subject.

Theosophists must have as a characteristic what we
may call an inherent yearning for self-knowledge in the
broadest sense. Even people only slightly familiar with
theosophy can sense that such self-knowledge will give
birth to a comprehensive appreciation for all human
feeling and thinking as well as for all other beings. This
appreciation must be an indispensable part of our whole
theosophical movement.*

Often people do not understand clearly that in our German theosophical movement what lights up our way is the

---

*For the sake of historical accuracy and to indicate the tone of the original,
we have not substituted or added "anthroposophy" where Steiner speaks of
"Theosophy" or "anthroposophical movement" where he speaks of "Theosophical movement." Nevertheless, the continuity between Rudolf Steiner's
theosophy and anthroposophy should always be kept in mind. (See note 1)

sign you know as the mark of the Cross with Roses. It is easy to harbor misunderstandings about our spiritual, theosophical movement that seeks to live into the spiritual life of today — that is, into our hearts and their feelings, our will and its deeds — under the sign of the Rose Cross. People easily misunderstand our movement. Many people, even those with good intentions, have difficulty realizing that our spiritual movement, working under the sign of the Rose Cross, is inspired in all its principles — in its whole feeling and sensitivity — to be understanding and tolerant of every human striving and every aspiration. Though this tolerance is an inherent characteristic of the Rosicrucian movement, it may not be obvious at first glance, because it lies in its depths. You will find, therefore, that people who confuse tolerance with the one-sided acceptance of their own opinions, principles, and methods are particularly likely to misunderstand our movement.

It is very easy to imagine this tolerance; yet to attain it is extremely difficult. After all, we find it easy to believe that people who disagree with us are our opponents or enemies. Similarly, we can easily mistake our own opinion for a generally accepted truth. For theosophy to flourish and be fruitful for the spiritual life of the future, however, we have to meet each other on an all-inclusive basis. Our souls must be filled with profound understanding not only for those who share our beliefs but also for those who, compelled by the circumstances of their own experience, their own path through life, may perhaps advocate the opposite of what we do. The old morality, now on the wane, taught us to love and to be tolerant of those who share our thoughts and feelings. However, with its truth, theosophy will more and more radiate a much more far-reaching tolerance into people's hearts. This more profound tolerance will enable us to meet others with understanding and encouragement and to live in harmony with them, even when their thoughts and feelings differ completely from our own.

This touches upon an important issue. What do people come upon first when they turn to the theosophical movement? What are they compelled to acknowledge first? Normally, the general insight people encounter first when they approach theosophy is the idea of reincarnation and karma — the idea of the continued working of causes from one life into the next. Of course, this is not a dogma for us. Indeed, we may have different opinions about this basic insight. Still, the conviction of reincarnation and karma forces itself upon us right from the start of our acquaintance with theosophy. However, it is a long way from the day we first become convinced of these truths to the moment when we can begin, in some way, to see our whole life in the light of these truths. It takes a long time for the conviction to become fully alive in our soul.

For example, we may meet a person who mocks or even insults us. If we have immersed ourselves in the teaching of reincarnation and karma for a long time, we will wonder who has spoken the hurtful, insulting words our ears have heard. Who has heaped mockery upon us — or even who has raised the hand to hit us? We will then realize that we ourselves did this. The hand raised for the blow only appears to belong to the other person. Ultimately, *we* cause the other to raise his or her hand against us through our own past karma.

This merely hints at the long path from the abstract, theoretical conviction of karma to the point where we can see our whole life in the light of this idea. Only then do we really feel God within us and no longer experience him only as our own higher self, which teaches us that a tiny spark within us shares in God's divinity. Instead, we learn to be aware of this higher self in such a way that a feeling of unlimited responsibility fills us. We feel responsible not only for our actions, but also for what we suffer, because what we suffer now is after all only the necessary result of what we did in the far-distant past.

Let us experience this feeling pouring into our souls as the warm, spiritual life blood of a *new culture*. Let us feel how new concepts of responsibility and of love arise and take hold of our souls through theosophy. Let us recognize that is no empty phrase to claim that the theosophical movement arose in our time because human beings need new moral, intellectual, and spiritual impulses. And let us be aware that a new spiritual revelation is about to pour itself forth into our hearts and our convictions through theosophy, not arbitrarily, but because the new moral impulses and the new concepts of responsibility — and, indeed, the destiny of humanity — require such a new spiritual revelation. Then we can know in an immediate, living way that it has a coherent meaning for the world that the same souls present here now repeatedly lived on earth in the past. We have to ask what this meaning is — why are we incarnated again and again?

We find this meaning when we learn through theosophy that every time we see all the wonders of this world with new eyes in a new body, we get a glimpse of the divine revelations veiled by the sensory world. Or, with our newly formed ears, we can listen to the divine revelation in the world of sound. Thus, we learn that in every new incarnation we can and should experience something new on earth. We understand that some people are destined by karma to announce prophetically what all of humanity will gradually, bit by bit, accept as the meaning of an epoch.

What people in the Theosophical Society — and in the theosophical movement in general — know because of these revelations from the spiritual world has to flow into all aspects of human culture. The souls living in this world now in their physical bodies feel drawn to theosophy because they know that this new element must be added to what human beings have already gained for themselves from the spiritual world in the past. We must keep in mind, however, that in every epoch the whole meaning of the mystery of the universe must be understood anew. Thus, in every epoch we have to meet anew what is revealed to us out of the spiritual worlds.

Our epoch is unique; though people often carelessly characterize every age as one of transition, this term — which is often just an empty phrase — applies in its truest sense to our time. Indeed, an epoch is dawning when we will have to witness many new developments in the evolution of the earth. We will have to think in a new way about many things. In fact, many people still conceive many new things in the old style and the old sense, finding it impossible to grasp the new in a new way. Our old concepts often lag far behind the new revelations.

Let me point out only one example of this. It is often emphasized—and rightly so—that human thinking has made tremendous progress in the last four centuries because it has been able to fathom the physical structure of the universe. Of course, it is only proper to highlight the great achievements of Copernicus, Kepler, Galileo, Bruno, and others. Nevertheless, this has led to an argument that sounds rather clever and goes roughly as follows. Copernicus's ideas have led us beyond the earth into space. In the process, what Giordano Bruno suspected has turned out to be true: our earth is only a small celestial body among countless others. And in spite of this, so the argument goes, we are supposed to believe that the greatest drama ever, the central event of evolution, took place on this earth and that the life of Christ Jesus is at the center of evolution. Why would an event of such great importance for the whole universe have been played out here on this small planet earth, which—as we have learned—is only one tiny planet among countless others?

This argument seems plausible—so much so that to our intellect it looks clever and intelligent. However, this argument does not consider the depth of spiritual perception revealed in the simple fact that the starting point of Christianity, the beginning of the greatest event on earth, is set neither in a royal palace nor any other glamorous place, but in a manger with poor shepherds. Clearly, spiritual perception did not content itself with locating this great event on our earth, but also moved it to a remote corner of the earth. It is small wonder, then, that this perception strikes us as odd and peculiar next to the claim that we cannot possibly continue to "have the greatest drama of world evolution take place in a provincial theater." (These words have indeed been used.) However, it is in the nature of Christianity to have the greatest drama of the universe take place in a provincial theater as well as elsewhere.

We can see from all this how difficult it is for us to respond to events with the proper, true perception. We have to learn a lot before we will understand what the right thoughts and feelings about human evolution are. Turbulent times are ahead of us — both for the present and for the near future. Much of the old is used up and worn out, and the new is being poured into humanity from the spiritual world. People familiar with human evolution predict — not because they want to but because history compels them — that our whole soul life will change during the coming centuries and that this change will have to begin with a theosophical movement that has a correct understanding of itself. But the theosophical movement must fill its role in this change with humility and with a true understanding of what has to happen for humanity in the coming centuries.

Only gradually and over time did people learn to study the structure of the universe with their intellect as Copernicus, Giordano Bruno, Kepler, and Galileo did. It was only in recent centuries that people learned to interpret the world intellectually — in earlier times, they attained knowledge in a very different way. In the same way, new spiritual insights are to supersede intellectual knowledge today. Even now, human souls in their bodies are already yearning to look at the world not just intellectually. If materialism had not done so much to suppress these spiritual impulses, such souls, in whom we can virtually sense the passionate yearning for spiritual contents, could appear even more. These spiritual impulses could then make themselves felt more strongly in people who are only waiting for an opportunity to look at the universe and existence in a different way than they did up to now.

Privileged people, endowed with what we usually call "grace," can often see in their minds' eyes what becomes the general vision of all humanity centuries later. As I have pointed out frequently, the experience of the impulse of the Christ event that Paul, an individual filled with grace, had on the road to Damascus will eventually become the common property of all human beings. As Paul knew through a spiritual revelation who Christ was and what he had done, so all people will eventually receive this knowledge, this vision. We are at the threshold of the age when many people will experience a renewal of the Christ event of St. Paul. It is an intrinsic part of the evolution of our earth that many people will experience for themselves the spiritual vision, the spiritual eye, that opened up for Paul on the road to Damascus. This spiritual eye looks into the spiritual world, bringing us the truth about Christ, which Paul had not believed when he had heard it in Jerusalem. The occurrence of this event is a historical necessity. This is what has been called the second advent of Christ in the twentieth century. Christ will be recognized as an individuality. People will realize that Christ has continually revealed himself by coming ever closer to the physical plane — from the moment when he appeared to Moses, as though in a reflection, in the burning bush to the time when he lived for three years in a human body. Seeing this, people will understand that Christ is at the center of earthly evolution.

A body has only *one* center of gravity; a scale has only one suspension point. If you support the scale beam in more than one place, you interfere with the effects of the law of gravity. A body needs only one center of gravity. That is why, concerning the central or pivotal point of evolution, occultists from antiquity to the present have acknowledged that evolution was headed toward one point, namely, the Mystery of Golgotha, and that human evolution began its ascent at this point. Still, it is very difficult to understand what the Christ event, the Mystery of Golgotha, really means for the spiritual guidance of humanity. To understand this rightly, we have to silence all the feelings and opinions from this or that denomination within us. We have to be as impartial and objective in regard to the Christian methods of education, which have prevailed for many centuries in the west, as we are regarding other religious methods of education. Only then can we really come to know the spiritual center of the earth's evolution. Nevertheless, in the coming centuries those who proclaim the spiritual central point of human evolution most fervently will be seen as "bad Christians"— or even as unworthy of being called Christian at all.

Many people find even the idea that Christ could incarnate in a human body only once, and only temporarily — for three years — difficult to understand. People who have familiarized themselves in more detail with what Rosicrucian theosophy has to say about this know that the physical body of Jesus of Nazareth had to be very complicated to accommodate the powerful individuality of Christ. As we know, one human being would not have been sufficient for this, and therefore two persons had to be born. The Gospel of St. Matthew tells the story of one of them, the Gospel of St. Luke follows the life of the other. We know, too, that the individuality who incarnated into the Jesus child we meet in the Gospel of St. Matthew had completed tremendous achievements in its development in earlier earth lives. At the age of twelve, in order to develop further capacities, this "Matthew-Jesus" individuality left its body to dwell in another earthly body — that of the "Luke-Jesus" — until its thirtieth year. Thus, everything humanity had ever experienced that was noble and great, as well as everything that was humble, worked together on the personality of Jesus of Nazareth so as to enable his body to take in the being we call Christ. We will have to develop a profound understanding to grasp what occultists mean when they say that there can be only one event on Golgotha — as in mechanics a body has only one center of gravity.

An epoch that faces great soul events, such as the ones we have briefly outlined here, is particularly suited to lead us to search our souls. Indeed, searching our own souls and hearts is now one of the many tasks of all true theosophists in the theosophical movement. We need to search our own hearts and souls — return within ourselves — to help us realize that it requires sacrifice to follow the path to the understanding of that singular truth of which the occultism of all times has unambiguously spoken.

Such times in which the shining lights of truth and the warm gifts of love are to be poured out over humanity also bring events confirming the truth of the proverb that "strong lights cast deep shadows." The deep, black shadows that enter together with the gifts we have just spoken of consist of the potential for error. The human heart's susceptibility to error is inseparably bound up with the great gifts of wisdom that are to flow into human evolution. Let us not delude ourselves, therefore, into believing that the erring human soul will be less fallible in times to come than it has been in the past. On the contrary, our souls will be even more susceptible to errors in the future than ever before. Occultists have prophesied this since the dawn of time. In the coming times of enlightenment, to which I could only allude here, the slightest potential for error as well as the greatest aberrations can gain ground. Therefore, it is all the more necessary that we squarely face this potential for error and realize that because we are to expect great things, error can all the more easily creep into our weak human hearts.

Regarding the spiritual guidance of humanity, we have to draw the following lesson from this potential for error and from the age-old warnings of occultists: We must exercise the great tolerance we spoke of in the beginning, and we must give up our habit of blindly believing in authority. Such a blind belief in authority can be a powerful temptation and can lead to error. Instead, we must keep our hearts open and receptive to everything that wants to flow out of the spiritual worlds into humanity in a new way. Accordingly, to be good theosophists, we must realize that if we wish to cultivate and foster in our movement the light that is to stream into human evolution, we must guard against all the errors that can creep in with the light.

Let us feel the full extent of this responsibility and open our hearts wide to see that there has never been a movement on this planet earth that fostered such open, loving hearts. Let us realize that it is better to be opposed by those who believe their opinion is the only true one, than to fight them. It is a long way from one of these extremes to the other. Nevertheless, those who take up the theosophical movement spiritually will be able to live with something that has run through all history as a seed sentence, a motto for all spirituality — and rightly so.

Upon realizing that though there is much light, the potential for error is great, you may have doubts and wonder how we weak human beings can find our way in this confusion. How are we to distinguish between truth and error? When such thoughts arise within you, you will find comfort and strength in the motto: The truth is what leads to the highest and noblest impulses for human evolution, the truth should be dearer to us than we are to ourselves. If our relationship to truth is guided by these words and we still make a mistake in this life, the truth will be strong enough to draw us to itself in the next incarnation. Honest mistakes we make in this incarnation will be compensated and redeemed in the next. It is better to make an honest mistake than to adhere to dogmas dishonestly. After all, our path will be lit by the promise that truth will ultimately prevail, not by our will, but by its own inherent divine power.

However, if our circumstances in this incarnation propel us into error instead of into truth, and if we are too weak to obey when truth pulls us toward itself, then it will be good if what we believe in disappears. For then it does not, and should not, have the strength to live. If we are honestly striving for truth, truth will be the victorious impulse in the world. And if what we have now is a part of the truth, it will be victorious, not because of what we can do for it, but because of the power inherent in it. If what we have is error, however, then let us be strong enough to say that this error should perish.

If we take this as our guiding motto, we will find the standpoint that enables us to realize that, under any circumstances, we can find what we need, namely, confidence, If this confidence imbues us with truth, then the truth will prevail, regardless of how much its opponents fight it.

This feeling can live in the soul of every theosophist. And if we are to impart to others what flows down to us from the spiritual world, evoking feelings in human hearts that give us certainty and strength for life, then the mission of the new spiritual revelation will be fulfilled — the revelation that has come to humanity through what we call theosophy to lead human souls gradually into a more spiritual future.

NOTES

PREFACE

1. When Rudolf Steiner gave the lectures revised for this volume, he was still connected with the Theosophical Society and therefore used the terms *theosophy* and *theosophical* when speaking of his own independent spiritual research. After his break with the Theosophical Society in 1912/13, Steiner used the term *anthroposophy* for this research and its results. For purposes of clarification the latter term has been added in square brackets each time the term *theosophy* is used in this book.

2. Rudolf Steiner, *Theosophy: An Introduction to the Knowledge of the World and the Destination of Man,* repr., (Hudson, NY: Anthroposophic Press, 1988) and *An Outline of Occult Science,* 3rd ed., repr., (Hudson, NY: Anthroposophic Press, 1989).

LECTURE ONE

1. For a further description of the essential differences between human beings and animals, see Wolfgang Schad, *Man and Mammals,* (Garden City, NY: Waldorf Press, 1977) and Rudolf Steiner, *Study of Man,* (London: Rudolf Steiner Press, 1966).

2. Steiner describes the aura in *Theosophy,* 140–153.

3. The physical body is the corporeal aspect of the human being, related to the mineral kingdom. The etheric body, or body of formative forces through which life unfolds, is related to the plant kingdom. The astral body bears desires, pleasure and pain, and the

qualitative world of emotions, and is related to the animal kingdom. See *Occult Science*, 21–28.

4. For a description of earth evolution, see *Occult Science*, chap 2.

5. Socrates, 470–399 B.C., Greek philosopher and teacher. Plato, 427–347 B.C., Greek philosopher, the most famous student of Socrates.

LECTURE TWO

1. Menes, c.3400 B.C., Egyptian king. First king of the first dynasty.

2. For a description of the planetary stages, see Steiner, *Occult Science*, 108–254.

3. Friedrich Wilhelm Nietzche, 1844–1900, elaborated his idea of the "superhuman" in the character of Zarathustra in his *Thus Spake Zarathustra* (1883). He portrays a future wherein humanity attains dominance and the realization of its earthly purpose through the free exercise of creative power. Nietzsche believed that modern spirituality is a symptom of decadence, and that the "superhuman" would triumph over declining Western culture.

4. Etheric body. See note 3, Lecture One.

5. For a description of earth evolution during the post-Atlantean epochs, see *Occult Science*, 229–254.

6. The Vedas are the most ancient of Hindu sacred texts. Steiner speaks of them in *Occult Science*, 231. Also *The Bhagavad Gita and the Epistles of St. Paul* (lectures 3 and 4) (London: Rudolf Steiner Press, 1945) and *The East in the Light of the West* (Blauvelt, NY: Rudolf Steiner Publications, 1986) 161ff.

7. The Akashic Chronicle refers to a pictorial record of every thought, feeling, and deed occurring since the world began. Accessible to psychic vision.

8. Kadmos, founder of the ancient Greek city of Thebes and its first ruler.

Kekrops, legendary king of Athens.

Pelops, son of Tantalus. King in Elis, father of Atreus and Thyestes.

Theseus, king of Athens. Conquered the Minotaur.

9. Johannes Kepler, 1571–1630, German astronomer, physicist, and mathematician.

10. Steiner here refers to a passage in Kepler's foreword to the fifth volume of his work *Harmonices Mundi* (1619), which reads as follows: "Yes, I am the one; I have stolen the golden vessels of the Egyptians to build a shrine to my God out of them far beyond the boundaries of Egypt. If you can forgive me, I will be glad; if you will be angry with me, I will bear your anger. Here I cast the die and write this book for today's readers as well as for those of the future — what does it matter? Even if it has to wait a hundred years for its reader: God Himself has waited for six thousand years for him who looks at His creation with understanding."

11. Scholastic thought was dominant in medieval Christian Europe from the 9th–17th centuries. Steiner describes the characteristics of scholasticism in *Eleven European Mystics*, (Blauvelt, NY: Rudolf Steiner Publications, 1971), 168–174. Also *The Redemption of Thinking*, (Hudson, NY: Anthroposophic Press, 1983).

LECTURE THREE

1. Zarathustra, 660?–583? B.C., Persian religious leader, also known as Zoroaster.

2. Brahman, Hindu Godhead or Absolute; the creator god of the Hindu sacred triad (with Vishnu the preserver and Shiva the destroyer).

3. The Rose Cross is the emblem of the Rosicrucians. Tradition associates the rose with Persia, the cross is the symbol of Christianity. Historically, the Rosicrucian Order is thought to have been founded as a secret society c.1430 by Christian Rosenkreutz. Commonly associated with healing, occultism, alchemy; Steiner counters the "... materialistic caricature of Rosicrucianism ... presented today. The task of the Rosicrucians was to formulate a

science by means of which they would be able to let their (universal) wisdom flow gradually into the world." *Rosicrucian Esotericism*, (Spring Valley, NY: Anthroposophic Press, 1978), 6. See also George Adams, *The Mysteries of the Rose-Cross*, (Sussex, England: New Knowledge Books, 1955).

4. Gnosticism arose in the Hellenistic era. Gnostics believed that salvation is attained through knowledge rather than through faith or deeds.

5. Arius, c.250–336, Greek ecclesiastic at Alexandria. Taught Neoplatonic doctrine that God is alone, unknowable, and separate from every created being, that Christ is a created being and not God in the fullest sense but a secondary deity, and that in the incarnation the Logos assumed a body but not a human soul. Growing dispute over his teaching led Emperor Constantine to call the Council of Nicaea (325) where Arianism was declared heresy.

Saint Athanasius, c.293–373, Greek theologian and prelate in Egypt. Lifelong opponent of Arianism. Attended Council of Nicaea (325) as deacon. Bishop of Alexandria. Advocated homoousian doctrine. Often exiled because of his opposition to Arianism. Wrote doctrinal works. Not author of Athanasian creed, which originated later (5th or 6th century).

6. Johann Wolfgang von Goethe, 1749–1832, leading German poet and playwright. *Faust* (1808–32), a drama in verse, is Goethe's masterpiece. The lines referred to are in Part Two, Scene 2.

7. Nathan and Solomon were both sons of King David, the second king of Israel. The Gospel of St. Luke cites Nathan as a forefather of Mary (Luke 3:31); St. Matthew traces Joseph's lineage to Solomon (Matthew 1:16). For a detailed account of the two Jesus children, see Rudolf Steiner, *From Jesus to Christ*, (London Rudolf Steiner Press, 1973), lecture 8.

8. The Zoroaster mentioned here by Steiner lived in very ancient times, according to the Greeks — already 5000 years before the Trojan war. He is not identical with the Zoroaster or Zarathustra mentioned in ordinary history.

9. Buddha, Indian religious leader, founder of Buddhism. Historical name Siddhartha Gautama, c.563–483 B.C. Some Eastern religions believe him one of the last incarnations of the Godhead. Son of a royal family, he renounced luxury and became an ascetic.

Bodhisattva, a being that compassionately refrains from entering Nirvana for the salvation of others.

10. Steiner describes the human being as comprised of four "bodies": physical, etheric, astral, and ego. The astral body bears the inner world of desires, pleasure and pain, and the qualitative world of emotions. See *Occult Science*, 21 –28.

11. Nicolaus Copernicus, 1473–1543, Polish astronomer. Made astronomical observations of orbits of sun, moon, planets. Gradually abandoned accepted Ptolemaic system of astronomy and worked out heliocentric system in which the earth rotates daily on its axis and, with other planets, revolves around the sun.

12. Giordano Bruno, 1548–1600, Italian philosopher. Arrested by the Inquisition and burned at the stake. A critic of Aristotelian logic and champion of Copernican cosmology, which he extended with the notion of the infinite universe.

13. See Lecture Two, note 2.

14. Nicholas Cusanus, 1401–1464, German prelate and philosopher. Bishop and later created cardinal. Wrote treatises for church councils as well as works on mathematics and philosophy. Anticipated Copernicus by his belief in the earth's rotation and revolution around the sun.

Galileo Galilei, 1564–1642, Italian mathematician, astronomer, and physicist. First to use telescope to study the skies. Tried by the Inquisition for supporting the Copernican system.

Further Reading

BOOKS BY RUDOLF STEINER

Christianity as Mystical Fact. Hudson, NY: Anthroposophic Press, 1992.

The Course of My Life (Autobiography). Hudson, NY: Anthroposophic Press, 1951.

Knowledge of the Higher Worlds and Its Attainment. Hudson, NY: Anthroposophic Press, 1947.

Mysticism at the Dawn of the Modern Age. Blauvelt, NY: Garber Communications, 1960.

Occult Science — An Outline. Hudson, NY: Anthroposophic Press, 1972.

A Road to Self-Knowledge and The Threshold of the Spiritual World. London: Rudolf Steiner Press, 1990.

Philosophy of Freedom (Spiritual Activity). Hudson, NY: Anthroposophic Press, 1986.

Theosophy: An Introduction to the Supersensible Knowledge of the World and the Destination of Man. Hudson, NY: Anthroposophic Press, 1971.

LECTURES BY RUDOLF STEINER

General:

Theosophy of the Rosicrucian. London: Rudolf Steiner Press, 1981.

At the Gates of Spiritual Science. London: Rudolf Steiner Press, 1970.

The Education of the Child in the Light of Anthroposophy. London: Rudolf Steiner Press, 1965.

Reincarnation and Karma: Their Significance in Modern Culture. North Vancouver, BC: Steiner Book Centre, 1962.

The Secrets of the Threshold. Hudson, NY: Anthroposophic Press, 1928.

The Spiritual Beings in the Heavenly Bodies and in the Kingdoms of Nature. North Vancouver, BC: Steiner Book Centre, 1981.

Christ and Christianity:

The Four Sacrifices of Christ. Spring Valley, NY: Anthroposophic Press, 1981.

The Gospel of St. Matthew. London: Rudolf Steiner Press, 1965.

The Gospel of St. Mark. Hudson, NY: Anthroposophic Press, 1950.

The Gospel of St. Luke. Hudson, NY: Anthroposophic Press, 1964.

The Gospel of St. John. Hudson, NY: Anthroposophic Press, 1962.

Building Stones for an Understanding of the Mystery of Golgotha. London: Rudolf Steiner Press, 1972.

From Jesus to Christ. London: Rudolf Steiner Press, 1973.

From Buddha to Christ. Hudson, NY: Anthroposophic Press, 1978.

The Fifth Gospel. London: Rudolf Steiner Press, 1968.

The Universal Human. Hudson, NY: Anthroposophic Press, 1990.

The Christ Impulse and the Development of Ego Consciousness. Hudson, NY: Anthroposophic Press, 1976.

Pre-Earthly Deeds of Christ. North Vancouver, BC: Steiner Book Centre, 1976.

"The Work of the Ego in Childhood: A Contribution toward an Understanding of Christ," lecture of February 25, 1911, Zurich: ms. available in the Rudolf Steiner Library, Ghent, NY.

Spiritual Guidance and Human Evolution:

The Driving Force of Spiritual Powers in World History. North Vancouver, BC: Steiner Book Centre, 1972.

Turning Points in Spiritual History. London: Rudolf Steiner Press, 1934.

Wonders of the World, Ordeals of the Soul, Revelations of the Spirit. Hudson, NY: Anthroposophic Press, 1983.

The East in the Light of the West. Hudson, NY: Anthroposophic Press, 1940.

Three Streams in the Evolution of Mankind: The Connection of the Luciferic-Ahrimanic Impulses with the Christ-Jahve Impulse. London: Rudolf Steiner Press, 1965.

Occult History: Historical Personalities and Events in the Light of Spiritual Science. London: Rudolf Steiner Press, 1982.

The Driving Force of Spiritual Powers in World History. North Vancouver, BC: Steiner Book Centre, 1983.

Ancient Myths: Their Meaning and Connection with Evolution. North Vancouver, BC: Steiner Book Centre, 1971.

Egyptian Myths and Mysteries. Hudson, NY: Anthroposophic Press, 1971.

Mystery Knowledge and Mystery Centers. London: Rudolf Steiner Press, 1973.

Rosicrucianism and Modern Initiation: Mystery Centres of the Middle Ages. London: Rudolf Steiner Press, 1965.

Universe, Earth and Man in Their Relationship to Egyptian Myths and Modern Civilization. London: Rudolf Steiner Press, 1954.

Lucifer and Ahriman:

The Balance in the World and Man: Lucifer and Ahriman. North Vancouver, BC: Steiner Book Centre, 1977.

The Deed of Christ and the Opposing Spiritual Powers: Lucifer, Ahriman, Mephistopheles, Asuras. North Vancouver, BC: Steiner Book Centre, 1976.

The Influences of Lucifer and Ahriman: Man's Responsibility for the Earth. North Vancouver, BC: Steiner Book Centre, 1976.

INDEX

DURING THE LAST TWO DECADES of the nineteenth century the Austrian-born Rudolf Steiner (1861–1925) became a respected and well-published scientific, literary, and philosophical scholar, particularly known for his work on Goethe's scientific writings. After the turn of the century he began to develop his earlier philosophical principles into an approach to methodical research of psychological and spiritual phenomena.

His multifaceted genius has led to innovative and holistic approaches in medicine, science, education (Waldorf schools), special education, philosophy, religion, economics, agriculture (Biodynamic method), architecture, drama, new arts of eurythmy and speech, and other fields. In 1924 he founded the General Anthroposophical Society, which today has branches throughout the world.